The 6-and-a-half HABITS of

Serious Lessons for Accidental Managers

JOEL HILCHEY

The 6-and-a-half Habits of Highly Defective Bosses

Serious Lessons for Accidental Managers

Written by Joel Hilchey

Cover Design by Sebastian Jaster

Funstitute Press

ISBN 978-1-0696395-0-9

Also by Joel Hilchey:

Brainsprouting - How to Become Fearlessly Creative & Have Better Ideas More Often

Teaching Creativity - Applying Brainsprouting in the Classroom

The Time to Climb

Learn more at

www.joelhilchey.com

To the bosses who aspire for "less terrible"

This book is shaped by your stories.

I'd love to hear your ideas, questions, & feedback.

Please, reach out:

bosses@joelhilchey.com

Contents

Introduction: Bad Bosses

It's often said that people don't quit jobs, they quit bosses. Anecdotally, that seems to ring true; nearly everyone has a story of some intolerable ignoramus who somehow ended up in management.

Of course, when deciding to leave a job, it's not just about the boss; the role matters too. But there's no question - a bad boss can make even a great job seem unbearable.

For nearly twenty years, my professional work has been in training and development; I specialize in working with leaders to improve workplace culture. Most people experience the dynamics of just a *handful* of organizations (and perhaps a dozen or so bosses) throughout their careers, but I've had the chance to interface with *hundreds* of organizations, including more than a *thousand* small teams. I've worked with front-line staff who *tell me* about their bosses. I've worked with the team leaders who *are* the bosses. It's been enlightening to hear all their stories.

As far as I can tell, most bad bosses seem to otherwise be fairly regular folks.

I fully recognize that it doesn't take much time hanging around other humans to realize that many "regular folks" are a tad annoying. We're probably *all* annoying at least some of the time. But "bad boss behaviours" run way deeper than regular "annoying habit" stereotypes like interrupting or chewing with your mouth open.

Even the most painful of bad bosses might actually be polite, kind, and productive in non-work settings. They're maybe even okay in some *at-work* settings! At the very least, they likely are (or were) effective in *some* ways, or they wouldn't have become the boss in the first place.

Employees often have *mixed* feelings about these terrible managers. People often share bad-boss stories that begin with some variation of: "He's a smart enough guy, *but...*" or "She's brilliant, and she's certainly built a good business, *but...*" Of course there are exceptions, but it seems likely that most bad bosses are actually relatively good *people.*

So how does a good person become a bad boss? I'm going to work from the premise that bad bosses are merely the products of bad *ideas.* They're likely trying to be *good* bosses but are either grossly uninformed or severely misguided.

Many new people-leaders don't get any training, but even if there *is* training, it doesn't guarantee boss-level success. Even well-intentioned management advice has the potential to create some *unhelpful* behaviours. Here's a basic example:

Suppose I told a new team leader that it was really important to "get people to finish their work on time." This seems like a reasonable bit of advice. But if I didn't tell them *how* to make that happen, they might resort to some annoying strategies. Perhaps they'd start micromanaging people. Or nagging. If that didn't work, they might start yelling or berating people. As the pressure mounted and the deadline approached, they could feel compelled to publicly call out underperforming individuals in an effort to assert their authority and bolster their reputation as a "make-it-happen" kind of leader. Maybe they'd end up taking over the work and just doing it themselves out of fear and exasperation.

Hopefully *you* wouldn't do any of that stuff, but it's easy to imagine that in an effort to do something positive (get stuff done on time), a time-pressured boss might inadvertently develop any number of behaviours that will consistently drive people nuts.

In my experience, there are a number of annoying habits that have weaseled their way into the dominant psychology of management.[1] Worse still, many people have come to view at least some of these off-putting behaviours as *desirable traits*!

Imagine again our time-pressured boss. Those annoying strategies (nagging, micromanaging, yelling, etc.) might actually have some success - at least in the short term. So you could imagine the new boss doubling down on those tactics. The poor fool may even (mistakenly) believe that their public, employee-shaming rants are the mark of an effective culture builder. Higher-ups may notice the productivity of the team and reward such results, even as the team members debrief their toxic office experiences with their therapists and plot their exit plans.

But whether a bad boss' deficiencies come from ignorance, arrogance, or are just twisted byproducts

---

[1] How many? Wait for it...

of noble intentions, we can hopefully agree that there are a bunch of ineffective habits that are far too common amongst management.

I've come to think of these as The 6-and-a-half Habits of Highly Defective Bosses.

Accidental Managers

The vast majority of bosses I've spoken with seem to have "stumbled" into their management roles. My anecdotal observations and conversations align with the research: The majority of people say they didn't get *any* formal training with their new roles and weren't prepared for the jump.[2]

These accidental managers didn't *seek out* a position of leadership - it's more like the role found them. They hadn't been angling for it. They didn't go to school for it. They didn't set out to manage people.

Some folks are entrepreneurs or founders of organizations. They didn't necessarily want to manage people - they were just gung-ho on *doing* a thing and then they realized they needed to hire other people to help get it done.

Another unintentional path to leadership starts with a skilled professional who mostly works independently - picture someone like a carpenter, or

---

[2] In fact, a study from Chartered Management Institute says a whopping *82%* qualify as these "accidental" bosses.

a pool service technician, for instance.[3] The story often seems to progress by happenstance: They found themselves extra busy in the springtime; their nephew was looking for a part-time job; the nephew brought along his buddy to help out… On it goes like this, and before anyone really realizes it, our "independent professional" pool service technician is managing a seasonal team of six, along with a half-time assistant and bookkeeper.

But just about *anybody* can end up in people-management roles. Countless folks start off in what they consider to be a "regular" job, working for a "regular" company, with no concrete aspirations of making the leap into management. It happens in literally every business.

Perhaps this was you? You started off as the person who was doing the work. You were serving customers, making sales, fixing engines, or doing whatever it is your company does. And then, at some point, almost unexpectedly, you found yourself in a position of people-management.

Perhaps you were a go-to technical expert. Or maybe you were the most senior person around the table when *your* boss moved on. Maybe you just happened to have a good relationship with a few of the new hires and it seemed natural for you to run the weekly meetings.

People are thrust into leadership roles for all kinds of reasons, but notably, many of them *don't*

---

[3] In my experience, even though these professionals *are* running small businesses, they often don't identify as "entrepreneurs".

involve careful career planning or management training.

It's not that these accidental bosses don't *want* the role - they often do - and they certainly don't want to be bad at it! Obviously they need training and guidance, but the *first* problem for these accidental bosses, at least in many cases, is that they don't even *realize* their role changed.

My Overdue Realization

I'm the CEO of a training company. We're a small team - five full-time and another dozen or so regular part-time contract staff - but we have an amazing and unique culture. People tell me that they like working with me, and on most days, I'm proud of how I show up as a boss. But frankly, this just means it's easy for me to juxtapose how things are *now* with how things were early on.

I became a boss without really realizing it, which feels a bit embarrassing to say, because "being a boss" feels like the type of thing one ought to notice.

I hired someone, and I guess that made me one of those "accidental" bosses. I mean, obviously I *knew* I had hired someone - that part was on purpose. But I didn't *feel* like a boss. In fact, the first time my assistant used the term on the phone, I bristled. ("Hi! I'm calling on behalf of Joel Hilchey, my *boss*..." **Joel* *shudders from behind his laptop across the kitchen table.*)*[4]

When I brought on my first full-time person, I didn't know anything about employment law, I just knew I needed help.[5] My wife and I had a two-year-old and we had twins on the way. We were run ragged. So, I threw together an online ad and happened to find a great person.

From my mostly-oblivious and naïve standpoint, it went along mostly okay for about a year.

Our training company was growing. We hired two more new staff members and we were already working with many contractors.[6] Then one day, my assistant came to me with an issue: Another team member had said some offensive stuff in front of a bunch of people. It wasn't *intentionally* offensive, of course, but it was the type of thing that mattered.[7]

My employee had fair questions, and I had sort of lousy answers. Paraphrased, it went something like this:

Do we have a code of conduct?

---

[4] For the record, although "boss" seemed *emphasized* to me, she said it quite normally. It was only awkward for me.

[5] Technically, I'd had a few part-timers previously. I had no written contracts, shoddy record-keeping, and in retrospect, I got very lucky that I had no major employment disputes.

[6] And I *still* didn't know anything about employment law... in the end, I was not quite so lucky this time.

[7] The details aren't super-important, but it involved religion.

No.
Should we?
Probably.
Do we have any policy for this type of thing?
No.
Should we?
Yeah, probably.
So are you going to do something about this?
Um.... yyyyyyeah.
Joel & assistant slow blink at each other

She wasn't upset with *me*, which helped. I was thinking and listening as fast as the hamster wheel in my brain would spin.

I asked some more questions. What did she want? What *should* I do?

We came to some sort of conclusion and made a plan. But for me, the power of that conversation was not in the specifics; it was in the *context*.

It dawned on me the next day while debriefing it with my wife: My employee was coming to me not just as "my assistant", but because I was "her employer".

She was coming to me because she was concerned about the team culture and her own *professional working environment*. She was concerned about the other people she was working with every day *and* the company's reputation.

So there I stood, after three years of leading a growing team, realizing for the first time that I was heavily responsible for someone else's *career*.

I was the boss.

The Research: Bosses Matter

There's plenty of research that says bosses matter. There's even *more* research that suggests there is lots of room for improvement. I'm not inclined to dwell on the stats and studies, but a few things are worth mentioning.

1-in-5 People Have Bad Bosses

Let's start with the big picture. Recent studies indicate that the majority of people - around 80% - are at least *somewhat* satisfied with their boss.[8] That's not terrible, but that still leaves about 20% - one in five - who are *not* satisfied.

So, even if you're happy with your boss, you likely have a relatively close friend who isn't. And that bad boss of theirs is messing up your friend's life!

Bad Bosses = Decreased Life Satisfaction

There's a strong chain that connects bosses with life satisfaction. Here it is:

It turns out "Job Satisfaction" makes up 25% of a person's overall "Life Satisfaction". That's big![9]

---

[8] The Pew Research Foundation study from 2023 found that about 80% of U.S. workers say their boss is excellent, very good, or good. The 2023 American Psychological Association published "Work in America" which found that 86% said they were "very" or "somewhat" satisfied with their relationships with their managers or supervisors.

[9] This stat is from a great 2020 McKinsey Article: The Boss Factor, with links to many more studies. 2020 was obviously a unique time, but the lessons remain valid.

The biggest driver of Job Satisfaction? Interpersonal relationships.

The most important interpersonal relationships? "Relations with management."[10]

The lesson? "Relations with management" are basically the *single-biggest factor* in someone's job satisfaction, and that makes it a pretty big factor in *life* satisfaction too!

The Specifics Support the Big Picture

The "roughly 1-in-5 people have bad bosses" stat has lots of related (and similarly-unfortunate) statistics.

For instance, roughly 12% of survey responders say the words *dismissive, arrogant, aggressive, and unpredictable* describe their boss "extremely or very well". That number rises to more than 30% when you include the "somewhat well" responses.[11]

Check out this laundry list of *desirable* boss traits. The percentage next to each trait is the fraction of people who say their boss is "poor" or merely "fair" at it *(i.e. not good enough)*:

- Helping them grow in their career. (28%)
- Setting high standards (19%)
- Being clear about expectations (22%)
- Giving employees credit when it's due (21%)

---

[10] In fact, managerial relationships are apparently about six times more important than "relations with coworkers". This was surprising to me, but underscores the impact of bosses - for better or for worse.

[11] That's also from The Pew Research Foundation study.

- Being open to new ideas (22%)
- Staying calm under pressure (19%)
- Making tough decisions (23%)

These percentages seem to cluster around 20%, so it might be tempting to think that one-in-five people have utterly terrible bosses who are "poor" (or merely "fair") in every imaginable way. But I'd bet this "poorness" is *not* concentrated in a few supremely bad apples. I think it's more likely that the negative traits are spread out amongst many (or even most) leaders.

Basically, bosses can be bad in a *variety* of ways, and being good in one way doesn't preclude us from being terrible in another. In all likelihood, almost everyone can do at least *some* stuff better.

Most People *Don't* Love Time with the Boss

One other discouraging fact is that despite the majority of people feeling at least *okay* about their boss, they still don't particularly like spending time with them.

According to Lord Richard Layard's happiness research, if you ask people to rate how happy they are at various times during their week, "time with their boss" ranks *least* happy.[12] While I couldn't find the specific source study to corroborate this, it *was* easy to find studies that put "paid work" very low on the list of activities. In fact, one 2017 study found that

---

[12] Lord Layard has solid credentials: London School of Economics, co-editor of the World Happiness Report, and a very long career. And also, he's called "Lord".

only "sick in bed" ranked worse.[13] And given that we now know how much bosses influence job satisfaction, I think it's fair to link bosses with paid work's low happiness ranking.

All this suggests (once again) that there's plenty of room for improvement.

Good Bosses Make Everything Better

Good management kicks off a bunch of virtuous cycles involving happier employees, more satisfying workplace relationships, more rewarding workplace culture, and better organizational performance.

Implementing "Total Quality Management" (TQM), for instance, has been known to improve results - both profitability and stock prices - since at least the late 1990's.[14] The goal is to introduce more reliable processes and systems to increase efficiency and reduce waste. Notably, managers need to engage *everyone* - customers, employees, and colleagues alike - in the quest. TQM produces good results, and it relies on *skillful* leadership.

There's also lots of research about how good "people-management" skills lead to better employee engagement and satisfaction, and those, in turn, lead to better employee (and organizational) *performance.*

---

[13] This is from Bryson & MacKerron: Are You Happy While You Work?

[14] This is from Easton & Jarrell: The Effects of Total Quality Management on Corporate Performance: An Empirical Investigation.

Think "employee engagement" is just a touchy-feely red-herring of a business metric? Think again. One study quantitatively measured that happier employees make more sales. In fact, they sell about 25% more for every 1-point increase on a 1-to-5 happiness scale.[15] This particular study looked at *natural* variations in happiness - not at the effects of good management - but once again, we've already made the link that good bosses make employees happier. Employee satisfaction also correlates with higher customer satisfaction, lower employee turnover, higher productivity, and higher profitability.[16]

So, there you have it. It's not an overstep to say it: Good bosses make everything better.

It's Not Easy

Being an effective boss isn't easy. Different people need different things from their managers. As the boss, you're responsible for juggling a lot of priorities as you guide your staff (and the company) towards success.

---

[15] The authors of the Saïd Business School study were able to determine causality here by leveraging a cool natural experiment: They had good sales data, and they figured out that employees are happier when the weather is good *and* they can see outside. They put it all together for their analysis.

[16] All summarized nicely in that "Boss Factor" McKinsey Article.

In fact, there's so much stuff to be responsible for that being a boss can feel pretty overwhelming. Between all the managing up and down the command chain, and all the reports (the "get me that report" *document* kind of report), and all the reports (the "you report to me now" *people* kind of report), even experienced managers have expressed that they need regular reminders about what's most important.

There's lots of worthwhile management training out there. There are thousands of great books about leadership.[17] But our discretionary hours are limited, and there's always some urgent fire that needs to be put out. Some months, try as we might, we just can't get to our ever-growing stack of "must-reads."

And even if we could magically know everything that's useful today, life and business keep changing, so the journey is *literally* never-ending.

In other words: It's really hard.

Why This Book?

Look, I studied engineering physics. I did lots of math.[18] I even got a Master's in environmental engineering that was broader in scope. I did a minor in business, so I learned about marketing and knew

---

[17] This number is a total guess... I haven't counted them.

[18] You may notice my affinity for math-y stuff as you read on, though I've attempted to keep it in the footnotes to avoid being that annoying engineer.

some stuff about accounting.[19] But I'll be honest: Even after all that school, I didn't really know *anything* about management.

I was an accidental boss, and I definitely could have used a fast-paced crash course before taking on my first employee. I didn't need to win the boss-of-the-year award; at first, I just wanted to keep my assistant happy enough that she wouldn't quit. I knew I'd mess some things up, but I didn't want to be terrible. Heck, I'd have even settled for *less-terrible*!

In writing this book, I heard some stories of *criminally* bad bosses... physical altercations, sexual assault, and even a harrowing story in which a woman overheard her boss threatening a "hit" on another human... (simultaneously realizing that her boss was part of the mafia...)

This book is *not* about *those* bosses.[20]

I wrote this book as a crash course for people like me: accidental managers who are out there every day with their teams, trying to do good work, and trying their best *not* to be terrible.

And to be clear, it's not just "new bosses" that need a crash course; I'd no-longer qualify for the "new boss" category, but as the meetings mount and the pressures persist and the complexity complexifies, I *still* feel like I need advice!

And I need that advice to be fast, because attention spans are short and distractions abound. I

---

[19] ...*knew*... definitely past-tense.

[20] But I did include those stories in the Bonus Round chapter near the end.

can hardly finish typing a paragraph without getting pulled towards... [21]

Simplicity, these days, is very helpful.

Brevity is good too.[22]

That's why I've designed this book to be the sort of thing you can pick up and put down. Bite-sized advice - each bit readable in five minutes or less. Keep it on your coffee table or in your laptop bag. Leave it by the toilet, if you like! This isn't War and Peace.

I've been working primarily with *people* for my whole career, but because I studied engineering, I'm drawn toward *tools* - especially tools that are simple and effective.

I wanted to create something to help people be *less-terrible* bosses - not by making a lengthy and nuanced argument for a new style of leadership - but by giving simple tools and practical advice.[23] Most of all, I hope this book can help everyone identify (and avoid) some of the big mistakes that plague even experienced managers.

---

[21] Note to self - find time to finish this paragraph in a witty way.

[22] I could literally write a whole book on the importance of brevity... volumes, even! But I won't.

[23] I know what you're thinking: "Not lengthy *or* nuanced?! Then I shall stop reading right here! Harrumph!"

What to Expect

Just so you know what to expect, let's talk through the way I ended up structuring this book. You've read enough by now to have a sense of my writing style, and hopefully my tendency towards tangents (which I try to avoid in my team meetings) can be mostly relegated to the footnotes.[24]

Content-wise, we're going to start off with a self-assessment, because everyone loves to know how they're doing against an arbitrary standard.

Then, I've given a very brief overview of the 6-and-a-half habits. Lots of folks only ever read the first 25 or 30 pages of a book before getting distracted and moving on.[25] So if that's you, at least you'll be able to reference the book and its main points in casual conversation. In other words, by giving you a summary of the main ideas early on, I hope you'll be able to impress your friends and colleagues who didn't get around to reading *any* of it.

After the summary, we'll get into each of the habits in more depth. It might be useful to know that there are a few common sections within each Habit.

One of those common sections is called *Complaints and Confessions.* Writing a book on bad bosses has had a bit of a snowball effect: Once people start hearing bad boss stories, others want to chime

---

[24] If you *enjoy* the occasional diversion, the footnotes may give you a glimpse into my brain. But you can skip the footnotes if you're in a hurry (or if, like my kids, you think my sense of humour is lame).

[25] No judgement. I do it too.

in. It seems cathartic and humanizing to share stories of trauma and less-than-human treatment. And sometimes, people have also admitted that they themselves have been a bad boss - that's the "confessions" part. Each of those bad-boss stories has great teaching power for what *not* to do. I've changed the details to make sure nobody gets more embarrassed than they already feel.

I've also included a section for each habit called Techniques to Be Less Terrible. While it's fun to complain, I thought it might be useful to share a set of "easy-to-do" tools and tips to help address the issues. Hopefully it won't seem overwhelming; five or six "tips" per habit quickly adds up.[26] Just start with the ones that feel most relevant (or most needed) and go from there.

I've wrapped up each habit with a short summary and a recap of the relevant assessment questions. Feel free to dog-ear those pages and keep the book by the toilet; every now-and-then you can open it up[27] and remind yourself of a few aspirational metrics.

---

[26] Or would it be more accurate to say they quickly *multiply*? I suppose that's another math technicality... But since we're being technical, let's estimate:

~5.5 tips & tools per habit x 6.5 habits

So we can expect 35.75 tips & tools in this book.

[27] ...the book... *not* the toilet. Or... well... *also* the toilet.

For Bosses & Employees Alike

In writing this book, I had a few specific goals:

1. **Develop Common Language:** Having a name for something helps people identify it when they see it. If you've got a highly defective boss, my hope is that this will empower you with some language on why they're so hard to handle. If these habits can become more recognizable, they should be easier to eliminate.
2. **Share Practical Tactics for Busy People:** People need tangible and usable tips, tricks, models, and ways of thinking that they will actually use in their roles as managers. Overall, I tried to write the type of guide that would have been useful for *me* to read in the early days of having a teammate, and then would be equally useful for me to *review* every so often.
3. **Be a Conversation Starter:** The ideas in any book die a short death if they're not discussion-worthy. To kill off these pesky bad-boss habits, we need to *not* kill the conversation. Why not try a quick opening discussion about one of the habits at a weekly meeting or reflective retreat? Or start your leaders off strong by including this book in your new manager training?

Whatever you do with it, I've put this book together as a tool for bosses and employees alike.

If you *have* a bad boss, hopefully this book will help you pinpoint what's so terrible about them.[28]

If you *are* a boss already, my hope is you'll never be the source of a story when someone mentions the old "People don't quit jobs, they quit bosses" adage.

My goal for this book is modest: Let's help each other avoid becoming the intolerable ignoramus.

---

[28] Maybe you even want to send it along to some colleagues as a gentle nudge? Or just leave it on the photocopier and hope someone takes the hint.

The Highly Defective Boss Assessment

Before we get to the habits themselves, go ahead and try out The Highly Defective Boss Assessment!

And since you're probably thinking about it, no the *assessment* is not highly defective. It's not even plain-ol'-run-of-the-mill-defective. It's a perfectly good assessment. Effective, we might say. In fact, I'd even go so far as to say that this is a *highly effective* highly defective boss assessment.[29]

And let's clear up the next question: No, "Unclear Assessment Titles" is not one of the 6-and-a-half habits.[30]

Anyway... When you're filling out the Highly Defective Boss Assessment (or as I sometimes call it, the Boss-essment[31]), you can either treat it as a self-assessment, or, if you're wondering about *your* boss,

---

[29] The word "highly" seems suddenly odd to me. Is it an adverb? Does one jump... *highly*? That jump was high... he sure jumped *highly*! But then again, I guess "effective" isn't even a verb... so I guess an adverb can also modify an adjective? That's cool! And "highly effective" is actually a "compound adjective"? Is that even a thing? Feels like it should be... I have high hopes that it is. I hope highly!

[30] Though perhaps I will inspire you to write a book about the x habits of highly defective authors?

[31] Feel free to use that...

just replace the "I" in the questions with your boss' name.

If you'd like to do the online version, go to www.joelhilchey.com/bosses - alternatively, go grab a pen!

Scoring Instructions

For each question, give yourself a score based on how strongly you agree with the statement:

4 = "Definitely! (Okay… 90% of the time.)"
3 = "Yeah, sometimes."
2 = "Not really."
1 = "Definitely not!"

Jot down your scores in the margin or on a scrap of paper. When you're done, add up all the numbers. Why not challenge yourself to do it in your head? Or, skip the mental math and use an adding machine.[32] Or once again, do the online version.

Your total *should* be between 21 and 84. If it's not, check your math.

Wherever you write your total, go ahead and put a circle around that final number… you know, to make it look official.

---

[32] You could even make a spreadsheet or a mathematical formula. *I* would think that was pretty exciting.

The Highly Defective Boss Assessment

1. I have time blocked on my calendar for both short-term tasks *and* long-term strategic planning.

2. I regularly check in with my team about their individual career development goals.

3. My staff would say I'm just as effective at managing interpersonal issues as I am at managing big projects.

4. My top performers are happy and motivated, and they actually *tell me* they love working with me.

5. I recognize and celebrate high performance without fear of making others uncomfortable.

6. My team would say we encourage excellence and challenge underperformers to improve, rather than lowering the bar for everyone.

7. I proactively identify and remove obstacles that frustrate my team.

8. I always set clear expectations and make sure my team has the tools they need for success.

9. I actively try to reduce the number of meetings and avoid micromanaging, even if I'm not sure what people are working on.

10. I intentionally give public recognition and credit - especially to the folks who work behind the scenes.

11. When things don't go according to plan, I step up and take responsibility and I don't shift the blame; it might have been someone else's mistake, but I'm the leader.

12. My team isn't afraid to bring up mistakes; when someone drops the ball, they know I'll help fix the issue without causing more tension.

13. My employees consistently respond well to my coaching and feedback.

14. I regularly ask for feedback, my team shares their honest thoughts with me, and I make sure I act on their suggestions.

15. I give feedback - even critical comments - in a constructive and emotionally-sensitive way.

16. My staff knows I care about them as people - not just about their work; sometimes they even open up about their non-work issues.

17. My staff tell me I'm kind and respectful, and they say they enjoy working with me.

18. Even though I'm the boss, people aren't afraid of me; they get stuff done because they understand its importance - not just because I said to do it.

19. My staff would say I'm highly reliable because I actually follow through on what I say I will do. (And if I don't, I apologize.)
20. I know that innovation is important but it can be messy, so I make lots of effort to create stability for our team.
21. Even when I have great new ideas, I try to avoid sudden changes to important projects; pivoting too fast or too often can create chaos.

TOTAL =

Your Highly Defective Results

Before I describe the scoring categories, I want to acknowledge the numerical oddities of your highly defective assessment results.[33]

Yes, there are 21 questions. It's not exactly a nice round number, but it's 7x3 - which is three questions for each category, so that was convenient.

---

[33] And once again, "highly defective" does not describe the *accuracy of the results*; it merely refers to the aforementioned boss-essment.

And yes, this boss-essment measures you on a scale of 21 to 84. You've never heard of a 21-to-84 scale? Don't judge me.[34]

And yes, if you've looked ahead at the ranges, you're correct again: The categories are *not* evenly sized. I get it... this thing wouldn't pass a first-year stats class. But this isn't *for* a stats class. It's to help you figure out if you are a terrible ~~human~~ boss.

Let's just look at the scores.

71 - 84 - Definitely Not Highly Defective

At least by your own self-assessment, you seem to be avoiding the big mistakes. If this was you, congrats - people probably don't hate you. If this was your boss, consider yourself exceptionally lucky. Should you still read the book? I'm biased, but definitely! Spread the good word!

56 - 70 - Probably Not Defective

On the right track with most things. Ask yourself if there's one area that needs attention (i.e. - a few questions that got 1's or 2's), or if the score resulted from being "pretty good" across the board. Life at work may not be perfect, but a boss

[34] We *could* have made each question on a 0-3 scale, but I worried that it would make it harder for people to be honest. Doesn't a "1" seem less insulting than a "0"? No need to further embarrass anyone who's already admitting their defects. Plus, if it were a 0-3 scale, then the maximum boss-essment score would have been 63. And doesn't that feel weirder than 84? I thought so too.

like this has a good foundation for growth, and can likely figure things out in a healthy way.

41-55 - Somewhat Defective

Scores in this range mean there are some big errors in several key areas. At best, things are mediocre. If this is you, people are probably noticing and complaining - if not to your face, behind your back.

21-40 - Highly Defective

Let's hope this was for someone who's not you. If it *was* you, don't worry - your secret is safe with me.[35] But also, you could probably learn a lot from reading. A score here means there are flagrant mistakes in nearly every area. If this was your boss, you'd best be on the lookout for a new opportunity.

Highly Defective Category Names?

You'll have to forgive the un-inspiring category names.[36] I recognize the high-water mark on this thing is "Definitely Not Highly Defective". And that's sort of like saying, "Not terrible". But here are three reasons I set the bar low:

1. I wanted to help people be *less* terrible. One book can only accomplish so much, but this felt achievable.

---

[35] I'm literally just a book.

[36] Well, technically you don't *have* to forgive them, but your grudge won't help you feel better.

2. This test isn't designed to measure whether you're doing a *great* job; it's meant to help you figure out if you're messing up big-time.
3. Whatever the category names, you shouldn't put too much stock in any one measurement. To *really* know how you are doing as a boss, you should probably ask everyone who works for you.[37] Too scary? Ask yourself what you're afraid of hearing, and then get to work on changing that.

Let's end this little self-assessment section with some good news: The fact that you care enough to have made it this far in the book probably means you're *not* completely terrible.[38] So give yourself a high five, because in all likelihood, you're at least decent, and a little effort will make you even better.

---

[37] Better yet, you should get those people to do an anonymous survey that gets submitted to *your* boss. And if you're at the top of your company and don't actually *have* a boss, have the survey submitted to your most trusted colleague. Or your spouse. Or maybe your mom.

[38] That's kind of annoying, eh? Probably the folks who *most need* this "how to be a less-terrible boss" stuff are the folks *least likely* to read it.

The 6 ½ Habits: An Overview that Comes Up Short

While this book is about the stuff that makes bosses come up short, we're all busy. So here's an overview that comes up short - but in the good (i.e. - not-too-lengthy) way. It glosses over everything.

Yes, we've sacrificed detail for brevity, so you may feel that these descriptions leave you wanting more. And that's a good thing, because then you can channel that deep sense of disappointment into the desire to read the rest of the book.

1. Function Forgetting

The habit of forgetting (or ignoring) one or more of the important tasks (functions) of being a boss.

As a boss, you're responsible for a lot. You need to balance long-term and short-term thinking. You must balance your time and energy between people-related stuff and task-related stuff. It's all-too-common to forget that *many* things matter: strategic planning, employees' career development, project implementation, and team relationships.

2. Mediocrity Mongering

The habit of holding back top performers and creating a culture of mediocrity.

Team unity obviously matters. Nobody likes feeling "lesser-than", but many bosses hope that they can save under-achievers some discomfort by limiting their high-performing colleagues and promoting a "good enough" mentality. High-achievers hate this, and if your actions consistently discourage and repel your top performers, you have a big problem.

3. Hassle Making

The habit of creating needless frustrations, rather than removing and preventing them.

Frustrations come in many shapes and sizes: Bad tools, unclear expectations, pointless meetings, micromanagement, and more. While there may occasionally be some good reasons for small inconveniences, engaged team members don't want to be slowed down. A great boss needs to recognize what's holding people back and dismantle the obstacles.

4. Credit Stealing & Finger Pointing

The habit of taking credit for other people's successes while dishing out blame for failures.

You need to have a philosophy about how to handle successes and slip-ups. Hoarding recognition is a sign of insecurity and makes people feel unappreciated and resentful. And while holding people accountable for their actions is a must, playing the blame game leaves people fearful, discouraged, and disempowered.

5. Feedback Fumbling

Being incapable of giving and receiving useful, encouraging, constructive feedback.

Employees need to feel that their work is valued, and they want to feel like they are growing and getting better. Bosses are responsible for much of this recognition and coaching, and they need to do it in an emotionally-sensitive way. Plus, employees will have feedback of their own, and a boss ignores this at their own peril.

6. Bully Bossing

The habit of using power tactics and fear to (supposedly) motivate results and get compliance.

Bosses who believe that power comes from being mean try to get things done by powering *over* their employees and bullying them into submission. But it's possible, and advisable, to take one's work seriously and hold people accountable while still being *kind.* Being a "tough guy" or "tough gal" boss *may* produce short term results, but it ruins relationships.

6½. Consistently Inconsistent

The habit of being too inconsistent to be predictable. By its sporadic nature, this habit is unworthy of a full number.

While society values visionary, entrepreneurial and charismatic leaders, too much change creates chaos. People need to know what matters most. Without a sense of grounding and predictability, employees can get frustrated and cynical - scrambling to accommodate last-minute whims and changes, and struggling to keep up in an ever-changing storm of larger-than-life ideas.

Habit 1
Function Forgetting

Most people over the age of 40 have heard of bifocals. I'm lucky to have never needed them,[39] but the bifocal lens is a pretty neat invention. The concept is that part of the lens is made to help you see things up close, and part is made to help you see things that are far away.

This dual-lens system is a handy-dandy tool if you happen to suffer from reduced eyeball-muscle function.[40] With bifocals, it's possible to see up close and way out in the distance pretty seamlessly while going about your day.

Whether you need bifocals or your wee-little eye muscles are still in great shape, this ability to *change* our focus is a great skill. It's helpful for our eyes, but an even better skill for our *minds*. In life, and especially as a boss in business, we need to be able to shift our focus.

The Main Job of a Boss

What is the main job of a boss?

While different companies may have different metrics (sales targets, retention rates, team

---

[39] ...at least, not yet.

[40] It's really wild to me that the iris is a teeny little muscle.

productivity, etc.), it seems fair to say that the difference between being a boss and not being a boss is that you have some responsibility for more than just yourself; you are at least somewhat connected to (and responsible for) the results of the *other* people on your team.

Let's make a bold statement: Your main job as a boss is to empower your team to do a great job.[41]

Hooray for simplicity! But obviously, in order to do a great job, people need lots of different things. They need support in a bunch of ways. So now the nuance can begin.

The Four Functions

Let's define two "dimensions" of the boss job.

As bosses, we certainly need to think about getting stuff done - the tasks - but we also need to think about our people. This "task-people" continuum is the first dimension.

If a boss focuses too much on the tasks and not enough on the people, they may end up with a highly productive team with a highly toxic culture. Everyone will likely be miserable. Of course, if you focus *only* on the people, you won't get anything done - hence the task-people tension this dimension highlights.

The second dimension is time-based; we need to look at some level of detail in the short term, but we

---

[41] This is probably disputable, but my pre-emptive argument is that 99% of the "roles" of a boss could be lumped under this umbrella category.

also need the ability to see the big picture in the longer term.

If a boss focuses too much on the short-term details, they can lose track of the bigger purpose and context. But if they *only* focus on long-term, big picture stuff, they won't be tuned in to the daily functioning of an office, and they'll struggle to turn big ideas into action.

If we put these two dimensions together into a 2x2 matrix,[42] we can define at least four "functions" that need specific attention from managers.

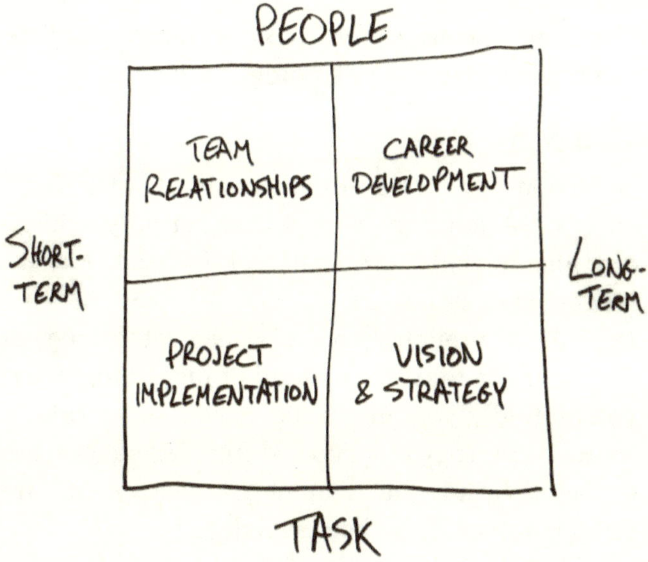

[42] ...which is one of my favourite ways of seeing the world...

Project Implementation

The Project Implementation quadrant is about helping your team do things well and get things done. It's short-term and task-focused.

This is probably the most obvious and comfortable place for managers to spend time, especially if they're a new boss, because it's most similar to what they were doing before. Even so, as a boss, you're probably doing more coordination and organization than you were as a non-boss "producer", and your focus may be slightly broader.

A guiding question for success here could be something like: "Are we doing things *well*?

Vision & Strategy

The Vision & Strategy quadrant is about making sure we're doing the things that actually achieve our bigger goals. It's still task-focused, but it's longer-term by nature.

This role is probably the next easiest for newer managers to take on. Instead of just "doing what you're told", you might be asked for strategic input, and that's a good thing. Managers are expected to have a broader perspective and are often involved in higher-level decisions.

A guiding question for this function could be: "Are we doing the *right* things?"

Team Relationships

The Team Relationships quadrant represents all the stuff that helps people effectively collaborate and have positive working relationships. Like project implementation, it's focused more on the present and short-term, but it's people-focused.

It might include basic things like introducing and welcoming new team members, but also involves more nuanced people-management skills. Bosses need to help resolve conflicts and make sure people on the team feel appreciated for their efforts. Plus, leaders need to ensure that the working dynamics are helping, not hindering, the team's achievement.

A guiding question could be something like: "Are people working well together?"

Career Development

Finally, the Career Development quadrant represents the talent-development and *personal*-development functions that bosses play. It's people-related, but long-term.

This is usually the function new bosses forget. Part of your job as a boss is to facilitate goal-setting and career-growth conversations. Sadly, very few new managers are given any real strategies to retain and nurture their people for the long run.

A guiding question for this final quadrant might be: "Are people fulfilled?"

People Usually Forget About People

Forgetting any one of these functions can be problematic, but there's a common path of pitfalls for new bosses. It seems to be most common that people forget to focus on the people-part of the job.

Fresh off a promotion to leadership,[43] many bosses double down on the "productivity" habits that made them successful in their previous roles. After all, this is often what made them stand out.

But being a boss requires more than just levelled-up productivity, and sadly, new bosses may not realize it until "people issues" start to emerge. The role of a boss is quite different from a pure "production" role; it's not just about managing people's *tasks* - it's also about managing *people.*

Balancing one's time along the first dimension (task-people) is often the hardest for new bosses to learn. If you focus only on the task-related part of the job, people will hate working for you. As the boss, you're responsible for creating the culture of your working team. Team dynamics matter a lot, and if you're the boss, it all starts with you.

A special mention needs to be made for the *long-term* people-focused duties - the career development stuff. Helping individuals with their career paths means having big conversations. You'll likely be talking with your direct reports about ideas and plans that will transcend your immediate team.

Some bosses might avoid these career-planning conversations because they subconsciously feel as though they're coaching their employees to *leave.* Don't worry about that, though. Your employees are thinking about career planning anyway. You can either be a supporter, a mentor, and maximize your working relationship by talking openly about it, or,

---

[43] ...or fresh into the stress of starting their own business...

you can keep your head in the sand and pretend they'll never go. People *will* certainly come and go, and it's part of your job to make sure the team can survive the changes. This is all a normal (if oft-forgotten) part of being a manager.

It's More than Multi-tasking

In all this discussion about the many functions of a boss, I'd like to note that I'm *not* advocating for being "better at multi-tasking".

Multi-tasking is the splitting of your focus as you attempt to do multiple things at the same time. And the short story is that it doesn't work too well.

Studies show that when we try to multi-task, we are *much less efficient* than when we're actually focused.[44]

When our brains are processing "multi-tasking" information, we aren't *actually* doing multiple things at once. In reality, our brains are just changing back and forth a lot, and we lose a bit of mental momentum with every subconscious switcheroo.

Bosses, then, have an interesting challenge, because there *are* a lot of competing things that need attention, but we need to be efficient and effective at all of them.

---

[44] Check out the consolidated research on Multitasking & Switching Costs on the American Psychological Association's website. Researchers say that even brief blocks and switches cost up to 40% of our productive time.

So I'm *not* saying that you need to constantly have all four functions rattling around in your head. I'm not arguing for unfocused inefficiency.

What I *am* saying is that you need to dedicate time in your schedule to focus on each function independently. They're all (at least periodically) worthy of your undivided attention.

Complaints & Confessions

"I once joined a team where the boss was great at getting stuff done but terrible with people. When I joined, a colleague actually pre-warned me: 'He's going to say a bunch of stuff that's semi-offensive and pretty critical. That's just his way. Try not to take it personally. If you can get beyond that, he's not a bad guy to work for.' I lasted for a few months, but that guy was a jerk. I left as soon as another opportunity opened up."

"Years ago I travelled with my boss and our team to a conference. After the evening reception, a group of us went to another bar - we were all younger back then. My boss obviously had *way* too much to drink, and then she disappeared with a man for a few hours before returning. She was a married woman. I don't want to sound judgemental, but it felt like she crossed a line. Isn't she supposed to be, you know, a role model or something? It's like she forgot she was the boss."

"My boss didn't really *do* anything. Technically we were a company, but it was more like she was leading a referral service. She didn't do the scheduling. She didn't do any training. She didn't help the team work together better. She certainly never asked me about my career aspirations. She was really lousy."

"I once worked for a startup. We dreamed big, and the founder certainly had a vision. There was always some new possibility on the horizon. We were a small team, and somehow this guy had got some startup funding, but to be honest, nothing ever quite materialized. I think the ideas had potential, but he couldn't get people rowing in the same direction. It was actually fun, because it felt like a permanent "strategy retreat". Except the founder kept shifting the target. After a few months with no concrete plans and no real development in *any* of the directions, I could see the writing on the wall, and I left. The startup folded a few months later."

"I once worked for an entrepreneur who had just started a small business. He hired me because he needed help, but he was incapable of clarifying any sort of strategy. He turned out to be pretty bad at delegation. He was always super busy, and I was too. We once spent three days trying to figure out how to fix the formatting on a website for a product that didn't yet exist. He spent another week developing detailed price plans for that same nonexistent product. We didn't have any customers, and instead of focusing on how we were going to make some sales, his attention veered wildly from place to place."

Techniques to be Less Terrible

Schedule Time for Each Function

Get recurring meetings on your calendar for each of the four functions. If you don't get them proactively on the calendar, you're not likely to magically find time at the "just-right" moments.

Think about getting the right cadence for each function. To clarify - when I use the term meeting "cadence", I'm referring to the meeting *frequency*, not the speed or length of the meeting itself.[45] For instance, you might think of potential meeting cadences as daily, weekly, quarterly, semi-annually, or annually.

Weekly Project Implementation Meetings

People need to be on the same page to work effectively. If your meetings are too far apart, you'll lose touch with what's happening on a day-to-day level. Weekly *might* be too frequent for larger teams, but monthly is probably too infrequent.

Not everyone needs to be at every meeting, but for the active projects, you likely need a relatively quick meeting cadence. The world can shift

---

[45] Although quicker, shorter meetings tend to poll better - so far the tally is: 2471 for shorter; 0 for longer. But that's just one survey.

quickly, and so can your priorities. Frequent connection times help people identify changes in the landscape and reprioritize urgent items.

Quarterly Strategy Check-ins

You can't get out of the "day-to-day" mode without trying. Longer-term, bigger-picture thinking requires setting aside specific chunks of time.

Your exact cadence with "strategy meetings" will probably depend on how much influence you have over your team's (and company's) overall strategy, but generally speaking, every three months seems to be about right.

To help underscore the difference in thinking you're looking for from the team, consider going somewhere different (retreat-style), or changing your routine (same place, but obviously not "just another day at the office").

Semi-Annual 1-on-1 Career Conversations

I suggest having two career conversations with your team members each year. In my experience, one of those will feel like a more significant conversation, and the other will feel more like a "check-in".

While not all businesses run on an annual schedule, many do. Whether it's related to seasonal work variations, summer holidays, or some budgeting schedule, most groups have some sort of *cyclical* calendar. As a result, there's probably a time in the year when your company (or at least your team) is planning for the year ahead.

It's often wise to schedule 1-on-1's with your team just *prior* to this annual planning time. Why? An honest career-development conversation will give you maximum information about your team members' goals and pending life changes.

Since it would be a bit weird to have a fulsome conversation about life and career goals and then go a full 12 months without ever mentioning it again, choose another time of year - somewhere around the six-months-later mark, to schedule a shorter check-in meeting.

Annual (but actually daily) Team Dynamics Check-ins

I find the annual career-development conversation is a convenient time to "formally" ask: Are there any interpersonal or team issues that I should know about?

By adding team dynamics to your annual 1-on-1 agenda, you'll guarantee it gets *some* attention. But, because we're responsible for handling shorter-term issues, you should definitely not wait until an annual review to address interpersonal problems.

As a less-terrible boss, you should pretty-much *constantly* be on the lookout for signs of potential issues. In other words, a sticky note on your wall or a *daily* reflection asking "how's the team?" probably wouldn't hurt.

Just like you wouldn't want a project to go for months without addressing some snag, you wouldn't want to leave people-issues unattended for any longer than necessary.

In my experience, people-issues often surface in private conversations (rather than full-team meetings). In fact, employees are often reluctant to bring up these issues at *all*. People who are dealing with tricky interpersonal situations usually care about being good team players; they don't want to throw their colleagues under the bus, and they don't want to be perceived as complaining.

This just means you have to work extra hard to get the truth and detect the issues. Observe carefully. Talk to your people regularly. Be open, astute, and ask lots of questions.

And when an issue arises, deal with it quickly, but not so quickly that you act unwisely.

Final Words on Habit 1

Function fixation would be only ever paying attention to *one* particular aspect of the job. Function forgetting is much more common, and it usually shows up as a boss who addresses a few areas "well-enough", but who ignores one or more key roles.

Perhaps a highly defective function forgetter is excellent at meeting metrics and building a team but avoids conversations about career-development. Or maybe they're fantastic at enrolling people in a big vision but incapable of articulating any action-items, so they leave people floundering in a foggy conceptual realm.

Meanwhile, the aspiring less-terrible boss will find time for *all* the essential functions. They'll shift their focus between short-term and long-term goals. They'll foster personal growth and functional team relationships. They'll effectively execute project details, but they won't get so tied up in the weeds that people lose the vision.

Don't be a highly defective boss. Get time on your schedule for all your important roles.

Don't be a function forgetter.

Reflect & Review

The relevant assessment questions for Habit 1 - Function Forgetting - were 1, 2, and 3:

1. I have time blocked on my calendar for both short-term tasks *and* long-term strategic planning.

2. I regularly check in with my team about their individual career development goals.

3. My staff would say I'm just as effective at managing interpersonal issues as I am at managing big projects.

Habit 2
Mediocrity Mongering

Let's talk about the Pareto Principle, or as it's more colloquially known: the 80-20 rule.[46]

The story goes like this: A long time ago, a guy named Mr. Pareto realized that some of his garden bean plants produced a *lot* more beans than the others. According to him, 80% of his beans came from 20% of his plants.

I don't know if most gardeners were in the habit of tallying up their green beans every day,[47] but apparently Mr. Pareto had a lot of time on his hands: He also had time to research Italian land ownership (80% of the land was owned by 20% of the people), then other countries' land ownership (same pattern), and then he kept finding more instances of this 80-20 thing.

---

[46] Observation: "Colloquial" is definitely not colloquial language. It feels like "commonplace" would be better. Except then my phrase would become: "...as it's more commonplace-ly known..." And that's obviously worse. English is silly.

[47] Though I heard some dude named Mendel (now known as the father of genetics) studied inheritance factors by counting his peas (in the pod) around the same time. Must have been a simpler era - everyone just hanging around counting vegetables...

Between all of his land-ownership surveying and bean-counting, I guess he also managed to spread his ideas around the world and get his name attached to the whole concept. That's no small feat, especially since he was born in 1848, which several sources confirm was before Youtube.[48]

Anyway, The Pareto Principle is generalized as "The Law of the Vital Few": 80% of the results come from 20% of the sources.[49]

If you do the math, this "law" doesn't always stick to exactly 80-20. Maybe it's 70-30, or 90-10, or 67-33. But the point is that it's *not* 50-50 (which is what it would be if everything were *equally* important).

So why am I bringing this up, you ask?[50] Because as a boss, you manage a team. And the results of your team are likely to follow the law of the vital few: Some people on your team will be exceptionally high producers.

---

[48] Actually, the more complete story is that Mr. Pareto's ideas didn't really get popularized until the 1940's. Another guy named Dr. Joseph Juran realized that industrial quality control issues followed the same 80-20 pattern: Most defects came from a few key factories; within a factory, most issues came from a few key workstations, etc. That guy popularized it. So now you know the deeper story.

[49] Mr. Pareto probably did a lot of other economist-related work too, but I'd guess that 80% of his reputation came from about 20% of his studies. See what I did there?

[50] After a page of explanation and ~~three~~ ~~four~~ five somewhat superfluous footnotes, you might add.

The message is simple: We must pay close attention to our top performers.

The Mediocre Many and Vital Few

Let's start by acknowledging that it sounds harsh to call the majority of people "mediocre". Allow me to clarify: It's not that *people* are mediocre, it's that their *skills* are. Everyone certainly has a zone of genius, and in an ideal world, everyone would spend the majority of their days doing the things they're really amazing at doing! But in *our* world, that's usually not the case.

Some people are in perfect roles for them, and they're really rockin' it, but probably the majority are doing, well... fine. It's not that the majority are *bad*, it's just that some people are consistently better.

These consistently-better, always-do-a-great-job, high-achieving folks are your go-to people.[51] You can probably rhyme off a list of these people without much thinking. If you're on a sales team, you know who brings in the deals. If you're in management, you know who you turn to for advice and insights. If your people work in customer service, you know who clients *love* working with.

A few of your team's top performers probably account for the *vast majority* of its success. Hooray for your top performers!

---

[51] Apparently, they're also well-defined by compound adjectives, which, I'm happy to report from the footnote back in the boss-essment chapter, are indeed a real thing!

But this comes with a small issue: Humans being humans, emotionally fragile as we are, we[52] sometimes get frustrated and discouraged when that uber-annoying superstar is so much better than us![53]

How to Handle the High-Achievers?

With all this as our foundation, now we get to the heart of the question for you as a boss: What is your philosophy about how to handle the varying levels of skills and performance across your team?

We can be even more targeted: How should we handle our high-achievers?

There are sort of two (or maybe three) options.

Option number one involves *encouraging* the high-achievers and helping them thrive. I'll call these people the Achievement Celebrators.

The second option involves *discouraging* the high-achievers. I know it seems like only fools would intentionally do this, but as we'll see, it's much more common than you'd think. Sometimes it's subversive. Sometimes it's explicit. But it really happens.[54] I'll call these discouraging folks the Mediocrity Mongers.

I suppose the third way would be to just *ignore* the high-achievers, but in practice, that will be discouraging, so we can lump it in with way number two. More mediocrity mongers.

---

[52] Yes, it's *all* of us at times.

[53] See? "Uber-annoying" - another compound adjective!

[54] That's why there's a chapter about it.

What Do High-Achievers Want?

Let's say you're an Achievement Celebrator, and you believe in encouraging and motivating your top performers. You're on the right track. But what do these folks actually *want*?

I have to say, I don't always *know* what motivates people. There seems to be a vast range of factors: Money, power, influence, recognition, relationships, stability, attention, achievements, creative control… the list goes on.

So while I can't say for certain what they *do* want, I think I've seen some important commonalities in what these high-achievers *don't* want:

- They don't want to be held back.
- They don't want to produce sub-par work.
- They don't want to be slowed down.
- They don't want their contributions or ideas to be overlooked.

Overall, I think we'd be safe to say that top performers probably *feel* their best when they're *doing* their best.

In other words, high-achievers don't want to settle for mediocrity.

The Mediocrity Mongers

We've all been on teams where we're one of the mediocre ones. And according to my therapist, I'm not the only one who feels kind of bad when it's me.[55]

---

[55] He's assured me of this *many* times…

So if we're the boss, it's understandable that at least a little part of us feels a bit protective of our mediocre majority. We don't want them to feel bad. We've *been* them. By most metrics, we *are* them. Nobody can be great at everything, after all!

But here's the problem: While we might all *feel* a bit protective, there's a subset of bosses who start to *act* a bit protective. They start protecting the mediocre majority by holding back the superstars.

Unless you've done some deep personal work, it's easy to revert to weird pithy lines you probably heard back in middle school when some cocky 12-year old was show-boating for his friends: *Don't be a show-off. Don't brag. What makes you think you're so special?*

I'm not a fan of boasting or show-offs who think they're superior to everyone around them, but here's the thing: High-achievers are usually *not* trying to show off. They're probably just trying to do good work. They're using their skills, they're in a good role for them, and they're being successful.

And sadly, just as these achievers are getting up to speed, a bunch of well-intentioned bosses start hitting the brakes.

What does mediocrity mongering look like? I think it shows up in three notable ways.

The Tall Poppy Syndrome:

Turns out there's some historical and geographical variation around this idea, but the basic concept is pretty universal: Cut down the poppies that are standing out. Poppy-chopping.[56]

In the workplace, you'd think that achievements would be celebrated. And sometimes they are. But apparently it's super-common for people to be resented, othered, criticized, or in-some-way "attacked" for their accomplishments.[57]

Not surprisingly, this is incredibly annoying and discouraging for those achievers!

Having a hard time picturing what this looks like? Just imagine a talented employee joining a team and quickly earning a promotion, winning out over several veteran employees. How would onlooker colleagues react to this news? Perhaps a healthy culture would celebrate their talented rookie with a round of high-fives, but in *most* workplaces, there'd be some cynicism. This could emerge as resentment around the water cooler or passive-aggressive comments towards the young star. That's Tall Poppy Syndrome in action.

Tall Poppy Syndrome might be rooted[58] in jealousy or insecurity, but it can also stem[59] from a totally valid belief in *equality*.

---

[56] One variation? In Japan, for instance, they use a harsher (err... less-flowery?) metaphor: The nail that sticks up gets hammered down. Want more? Check out the Wikipedia article on Tall Poppy Syndrome - it has links to the other global variants of this idea.

[57] According to Rumeet Bilan, over 90% of women deal with it, but she emphasized that it wasn't *just* women.

[58] Hah!

[59] Hah again!

This can get complex, but let's acknowledge that "promoting achievement" is sometimes at odds with "promoting equality". Even the *fairest* of meritocracies will have some people at the bottom, and those people often feel resentful for their position. To remedy this, it's common (and wise) to give *some* extra support to those at the bottom. That promotes the value of equality. But, if the folks at the top start feeling like they're receiving so *little* support (relative to the others) that they're basically being "punished" (poppy-chopped) for being successful, then they'll *also* start feeling resentful.

Basically, every culture needs to find the balance: promote equality and support those who need it, all without discouraging the high-achievers.[60]

The Good Enough Mentality:

High-achievers are usually interested in doing a *great* job. They'll be de-motivated by a boss who

---

[60] Want another example to showcase the complexity of this idea? Most of us feel at least a small pang of resentment towards billionaires. Or perhaps jealousy? Or maybe we feel that a billionaire's financial success means they wouldn't understand the "real" issues of "real" people. Note the "othering" that has emerged... I certainly believe in progressive taxation - where the wealthy pay more - but I have to admit progressive taxation is a form of Tall Poppy Syndrome. So even as I am writing to *discourage* Tall Poppy Syndrome in the workplace, I can certainly empathize with its roots - especially at the societal level.

says things like, "Well aren't *you* being fussy!" Or, "Slow-down! That's good enough!"

There are certainly *instances* where a "good enough" mentality is wise. We need to pick our battles in life. Perfectionism can be debilitating. As the saying goes, "There's only so many hours in a day."[61] Sometimes we need something that works "well-enough", but we need it *now*. And hey, if the astronauts on the International Space Station are using duct tape to fix stuff way up there, then who am I to judge?[62]

But most times, a "good enough" mentality is *not* particularly wise.[63] We want to encourage innovation and high quality and continual improvement. And we want to keep our high-performers happy, and they want to fly!

So beware, because if you lean in too hard on the laissez-faire, "it's fine" type culture, your best folks probably won't really dig it.

The Risk-Aversion Trap:

Managers are often in a position of quality control, which drives them to take fewer risks. Obviously

---

[61] That's a weirdly non-specific expression, eh? Like, we *know* how many hours there are… and "so many" makes it sound like there's kind of a *lot*. I vote we change it: "There's only 24 hours in a day." No? Okay fine… the current one is probably (wait for it…) good enough.

[62] They *actually* do this. Fixing a spaceship with duct tape intuitively sounds *insane* to me. So *fine*… I *am* judging.

[63] Like… for instance… maybe when you're on a spaceship?!

reliability and predictability have their benefits, but there are also *costs* to this risk aversion.

Top performers are often looking for creative ways to improve. That's good! But by definition, creativity chases new and original ideas, which means the outcomes become more uncertain.

Typically, the more senior the position, the more responsibility the individual has, and so the higher the stakes seem to be. Some managers are so risk-averse that they start to view everything as a high-stakes test. They feel like any minor slip-up will reflect badly on them and the organization.

When a boss is uncomfortable with uncertainty or risk, creativity and innovation get squashed. More importantly for those high-achieving employees, autonomy and motivation plummet as fear paralyzes independent decision-making, experimentation, and risk-taking. Mediocrity will prevail.

So, there you have it. If you are actively discouraging your top performers - poppy chopping, or promoting a general "doesn't really matter" sort of culture, or if you're so risk-averse that you discourage creativity, you are mediocrity mongering. And if you're doing that, you're about to have a big problem: Your highest-performing folks will probably quit.[64]

---

[64] On the positive side, at least you won't have to worry about anyone feeling badly about under-achieving anymore... at least, not until *your* bosses (or your customers) see your team's uninspired results.

Complaints & Confessions

"My boss actually once said: 'Slow down - you're making the rest of us look bad.' I thought that was just a thing people sort of pretended to say as a joke when they were pretending to be insecure."

"One of my people seems a bit upset that he's not getting assigned to more interesting projects, and I have to admit that I'm not totally sure how to handle it. He's not our go-to guy, but I don't think *he* knows that, and I haven't really found a good way to level his expectations and acknowledge that he's not *bad*, but he's just not our go-to. We use him for specific projects, and I try to be kind, but I feel like I mostly just try to avoid talking about our superstar teammates and their interesting projects while our 'rank-and-file' folks like him are around."

"I worked as an electrician, and when I was an apprentice, my mentor specifically taught us that even if nobody saw our work, it was worth doing it right. But then one of my first supervisors had this annoying phrase: 'If the customer doesn't see it, it's not worth our time.' A lot of our work gets covered up with drywall, so I get what he was saying, but it really went against my professional intuition."

"On one of my consulting teams, this one woman would always say these ridiculous lines. Stuff like: 'We're not trying to reinvent the wheel, here!' and 'Let's just keep it simple, stupid!' I was trying to pitch out-of-the-box ideas, but I always felt like a bit of a fool because this woman would just shoot them all down. She wasn't even the team lead, but the big boss never said anything to counteract her or show even a *little* support for any creative thinking, so I think she ended up dominating the culture. I ended up moving cities when I got married, and honestly, I was happy to change offices."

"I'm not trying to bash unions or overgeneralize here, but everyone at my plant, *including* the non-unionized managers, seemed to have this story about how we "union-folks" shouldn't work too hard. It was *so* weird. Our managers actually seemed more interested in 'policing' us to make sure we *didn't* work too hard. No idea if anyone ever put in "extra effort"... it probably would have been tough to pull off."

Techniques to be Less Terrible

Keep Your Superstars

Every team has members that deliver huge results. Of course, nobody can win the championship singlehandedly, but it's exceptionally rare to have championship teams without *some* superstars.

These key players "get it, want it, and have the capacity to do it."[65] They're insightful, productive, and they consistently "wow" people. Do what it takes to keep these high-achievers on your team.

---

[65] This is the approach suggested in the book Traction, which defines EOS - Entrepreneurial Operating System.

Consistent rules and policies are often meant to encourage conformity and ensure everyone maintains a *minimal* standard. And obviously it's good to have clear expectations. However, it might be worth reconsidering your policies if they are holding back your key people, discouraging them, or driving them away.

Fairness is a nice goal, but you probably make exceptions for individuals all the time anyway. Get creative with compensation, flexibility, working arrangements, or anything else that makes it easier to retain those big producers.

I recognize that union environments can be extra challenging for this. Often there are rules that make it difficult (or impossible) to be flexible or to reward top performers. In these cases, social recognition and informal approaches become doubly important.[66]

Water the Tall Poppies

Instead of chopping down the tall poppies, water them. Success should be celebrated, not belittled or attacked.

In other words, when you want something to grow and flourish, add fertilizer.[67]

Build a metaphorical fence around these achievers to keep them focused on their highest-value

---

[66] Your top performers are still human, after all, and they'll likely respond very well.

[67] I recognize that it sounds a bit like I am advocating for dumping poop on your high-achievers. I'm not. It's a metaphor.

activities. Defend them if they're attacked. Encourage them. Give them recognition.

Celebrate Unique Talents

Your team's culture will respond to what the leader values. If you value conformity, that's what you'll get, and it will be discouraging for your top performers - they usually want to stand out and be recognized.

Instead, celebrate the unique talents and contributions of each member of your team. The top performers will thrive in this type of culture. But just as importantly, the "mediocre many" won't have to feel so "mediocre" because they'll be receiving recognition for their *unique* contributions.

Successful teams *do* have superstars, but not everyone *needs* to be a top-scorer. The best teams are made up of a diversity of people and talents - all of which are worthy of celebration and recognition.

A great boss, like a great coach, builds on the foundation of respect and appreciation for *all* the contributions, and then figures out how to help people complement each other. Synergy helps the team achieve more than any individual could on their own.

The "Enthusiastically Re-hire" Test

Every now and then, ask yourself a simple question about each of your team members: "Knowing what I know now, would I enthusiastically re-hire this person for their current position?"

If the answer is "no," make a plan, and fast.

Are they coachable?

Could you find a replacement?

Could you shift their role to better align with their strengths?

Many of your "A" players are likely frustrated by the need to work with B & C players who slow them down. So even if that sub-par employee is "adequate" in their current role, doing nothing will implicitly nudge your team towards mediocrity.

The SFD - "Crappy" First Draft

There are times when "good enough" really is "good enough". To help clarify when you *want* something to be unpolished or unfinished, it's helpful to give your team some language.

I suggest the "SFD" - which is an acronym for "Crappy First Draft".[68]

When you want a rough draft of something, tell your team you want an SFD. This implicitly juxtaposes this particular project with your usual expectations, which would (hopefully) be of higher quality.

---

[68] Yes, I recognize the letters don't quite match. Use your imagination. "Crappy" already feels like it's flirting with the line of decorum. My colleague Brandon Love and I came up with this concept (and almost-correct acronym) several years ago. We later learned that Anne Lamott also uses this language in her treatise on how to write: Bird by Bird.

Final Words on Habit 2

Mediocrity Mongering has noble roots: a boss who wants to protect the egos of team members who genuinely can't keep up with the superstars. Well… that, or maybe it starts with a boss who's just kind of lazy.

The problem is that high-achievers are statistically responsible for a *huge* part of the team's success, and they don't like feeling held back.

Highly defective mediocrity mongers are content to cut down outstanding achievements, celebrate the status quo as "good enough", and avoid even moderately-risky prospects.

The aspiring less-terrible boss knows that keeping the superstars happy and motivated produces outsized results. Less-terrible bosses will celebrate the unique talents of the team while also taking steps to insulate the high-achievers from ho-hum colleagues.

Don't be a highly defective boss. Create a culture that nurtures and supports high-achievers.

Don't be a mediocrity monger.

Reflect & Review

The relevant questions for Habit 2 - Mediocrity Mongering - were 4, 5, and 6:

4. My top performers are happy and motivated, and they actually tell me they love working with me.

5. I recognize and celebrate high performance without fear of making others uncomfortable.

6. My team would say we encourage excellence and challenge underperformers to improve, rather than lowering the bar for everyone.

Habit 3
Hassle Making

There is perhaps no stronger stereotype of bureaucratic nonsense than the thought of renewing one's driver's license.

The process, at least in my mind, will play out something like this:

I'll show up at the office, see a line of perhaps eight people, and pat myself on the back for choosing a not-too-busy time. After grabbing a little paper number thing, I'll stand in the line for a surprisingly long time. (I'll distract myself by noticing the layer of dust on the fake plants. I might even guesstimate the number of weeks since someone last dusted.) At the 37-minute mark, my mind will turn to the more pertinent question of how a line of only eight people could possibly be moving so slowly.

Eventually, my number will come, and I'll finally hand over my envelope of renewal papers. After six minutes of watching them manually type in all the information, I might ask some innocent and half-joking question about whether the government might already have *had* this information in their computer system from the *last* time I renewed the license. But I imagine the clerk not having much of a sense of humour about it.[69]

Inevitably, they'll inform me that I'm missing a validation sticker of some sort (it was supposedly mailed about three and a half years ago), and I'll be sent home to look for it.

I'll leave feeling frustrated, but then, after a few hours of leafing through various file folders and unsorted piles on my desk, I'll actually *find* the dumb sticker.

I'll rush back to make it before 5pm, only to find that it actually closed at 4pm. I'm busy the next day, which is the Friday before the long weekend, so they'll re-open on Tuesday.

After another week of mostly forgetting about it (and one time remembering at 3:57 that I meant to get back there before 4), I'll finally make it back, sticker-in-hand. I'll wait in the line again, my mind pondering a range of newly observed peculiarities ("Why the heck do they have *both* a line *and* a "take a number" thingie?") and I'll likely find myself a bit agitated when my number is finally called.

My stress levels rise again as I overhear the young man at the next kiosk: "What do you mean I need two forms of ID to get a license? I don't *have* ID. That's why I need a license!"

---

[69] I imagine this person to have the demeanor and attitude of Patty & Selma Bouvier - Marge's chain-smoking sisters from The Simpsons. They actually *did* work at the Springfield Department of Motor Vehicles, so that might be influencing me.

The agent at my counter brings me back to my situation: "How can I help you today?"

I tell her I need a renewal and hand over my envelope. She spends another six minutes typing in my info. ("What could possibly be taking so long about typing my license information? Is there an essay part of this application?") I try the same joke: "You'd think the government would have that stuff from the last time I renewed, eh?"

But this time I get a serious response: "When was the last time you renewed?"

"Oh... um. I don't know, actually. Four years ago? Five? Well actually I guess *technically* I was here about two weeks ago. I just didn't have the sticker so they couldn't complete it." I shuffle through the papers on the counter and give the sticker a little wave.

"You were? You should have said that before. You'll have an open-renewal started in our system already... Yes... Here it is. Give me a minute to delete the one I just started."

"Okay. Sure."

She looks at her screen a bit longer. "You said you renewed five years ago?"

I'm getting confused. "I actually don't remember. It was a whole different office back then. Does my renewal date even matter? Is it listed on my current license? Wait... don't *you* have that information?"

She looks at the screen some more: "Yes - I can look it up - it'll just take a minute or two."

She starts typing and scrolling, and she seems friendlier than the person last week, so I hold my tongue, satisfying myself instead to rant silently in my mind. ("How can it possibly take two minutes to look up *anything*? Are these computers still on dial-up? Should I just look on my phone? Honestly, I could probably find the event in my calendar history in like, 10 seconds…")

She hands me an 8.5"x11" sheet from the printer. "Here's your temporary license. Keep this with you until you get the new one in the mail."

I fold the thing four times. "They don't have anything smaller, eh?" I feel the page crumple and then rip as I shove it into my already overstuffed wallet.

Once again, she doesn't see the humour. "Try to keep it from getting wrinkled - it's an official government document."

"Okay." I lie. "Do you need this sticker now?"

"Well... Good news!" She chirps. "You actually renewed *three* years ago."

"Okay…"

"The requirements changed a few years ago - you know - to streamline things. You actually *don't* need that sticker!"

Nobody Likes a Hassle

Clearly, I have a chip on my shoulder about license renewals. You're probably annoyed at the hassle of even *reading* about it. You didn't even have to *experience* it and it sucked!

So why did I feel compelled to write a three-page scene of an imaginary bureaucratic nightmare-ish nuisance?

Because hassles are bad. Even the *thought* of them is enough to boil my blood.[70]

I don't think I'm alone in my distaste for hassles. Hassles are, by definition, unwanted and unnecessary. You can probably think of a laundry list of stuff in life and work that seems to be pointless, frustrating, or unnecessarily complicated.

In fact, go ahead and think of it now! I'll even give you a bit of space to journal about it. Get it out on paper - it's cathartic!

-
-
-
-
-
-
-

Isn't that stuff annoying? Thought so.

Here's the key thing to realize: *Nobody* likes a hassle.

So let's bring this conversation back towards the world of work and bad bosses.[71] Hassles *at work*

---

[70] I recognize that I could have saved you the hassle of reading the story and just *told* you that hassles are bad... but I wanted this to be an experiential lesson. Sorry about that. I hope it's memorable and also that you forgive me.

[71] Though I might start a writing group to share stories of the hassles we experience as consumers. This really *was* helpful for me. Thank you for listening.

are especially discouraging. We navigate more than enough annoying bureaucracy in our personal lives; at work, we want to feel like productive contributors.

Defective bosses don't realize the hugely negative impact that "small" hassles have on their employees' overall psyche and productivity. These hassles are especially repulsive for top performers - the very folks good bosses should be trying extra hard to keep around.

Instead of adding needless frustration, great leaders will *de-hassle* their people. Let's talk about three specific hassles that bosses should help their people avoid.

Hassle #1: Bad Tools

If you've seen the 1999 movie Office Space, you'll remember the classic "printer-beating in the field" scene.[72] If you haven't seen it, the basic summary is that after years of pent-up frustration with their malfunctioning office printer, the three disgruntled and soon-to-be-fired employees take out their aggression on the thing with a baseball bat.

It hopefully goes without saying that I'm not *endorsing* this behaviour, but the scene remains a

---

72 Incidentally, if you have *not* seen Office Space, you should. The script could probably serve as an appendix to this book.

cultural meme because it tapped into a deep and universal anger: "Tools that don't... f-ing... work."[73]

While *your* anger may not have reached such epic proportions (yet?), if you've ever tried to do a job with shoddy tools, you're likely well-aware of the fury it can ignite.

Electronic equipment is probably the example that's most readily available: Outdated computers, malfunctioning photocopiers, wifi connectivity problems, tangled or "hanging-by-a-thread" cables... it all conjures up vague scenes of overly frustrated people slapping and banging their hands on the cases of sensitive equipment in a last-ditch attempt to make it work.

There's perhaps another category of e-frustration: not having the proper permissions. There's obviously good reasons for security settings, but I think it's fair to acknowledge that human shoulders get a little slumpier every time someone gets the dreaded "Access Denied: Speak to Your Network Administrator" error.

Though it may seem a bit ethereal, information itself could be thought of as a "tool". When bosses don't give their people the information they need, teams get frustrated. People may end up sitting around, just *waiting*, paralyzed by the need for answers. It's a colossal waste of everyone's time.

---

[73] These are obviously not *my* words... I wouldn't speak like this personally, of course, and it's not like I needed to write a whole book just to look for validation on my lingering "bad tool frustration." No no... This is a quote from... umm... another guy I knew.

But bringing it back to the physical realm, good tools matter hugely. For those in the skilled trades who work with their hands, the tools are an essential part of quality workmanship. And any semi-handy hobbyist knows that trying to use the nearby wrench as a makeshift hammer will likely end up causing more problems than it solves. In fact, I have a theory that having access to the right tools (and knowing how to use them well) is one of the things that makes a professional so much more effective than a hobbyist.

The truth is that almost *every* job has a bunch of specialized equipment. And if people don't have it - if they are working with *bad* tools, they work less effectively, less efficiently, and they probably feel pretty darn terrible in the process.

Hassle #2: Fuzzy Expectations

It may seem obvious to say that people need clear expectations, but it needs to be said precisely for that reason: It seems so obvious that it's often overlooked.

Managers need to guide a team toward a common goal. If roles, goals or guidelines are unclear or misunderstood, people fumble through their jobs, work inefficiently, and waste time and energy.

Suppose Sally tells Doug that a project needs to be done by Friday. Doug responds with a cheerful, "That sounds great!"

Both Sally and Doug may *feel* perfectly clear in what has just been communicated. But an astute onlooker might note that "by Friday" has multiple meanings, and the two colleagues could be headed towards a conflict and a major hassle.

Doug may assume that Sally needs the project done by the end-of-day on Friday. Sally, on the other hand, may have actually meant that she needs the project done *for* Friday - perhaps she has an important meeting in the morning.

Alternatively, Sally may have assumed that by telling Doug about the project and deadline, it was clear that Doug himself needed to *do* this project. Meanwhile, Doug may have assumed that he was merely being kept in the loop. Perhaps Doug believed his part was already done and the project was now in Sally's court.

"By Friday" isn't crystal clear at all. Who is doing it? What's the next action? What constitutes "done"?

Fuzzy expectations are especially problematic in a hierarchical workplace. Here, people may be afraid to ask for clarity because they fear it will expose them as incompetent. Sadly, in this situation, the real incompetence is coming from management. Defective bosses tend to offer too little clarity upfront, and this creates hassles through the whole process.

Here are a few sub-categories of fuzzy expectations:

Fuzzy Roles can lead to two separate hassles: First, some people may double up on work that someone else is also doing. Second, fuzzy roles might cause important tasks to get missed entirely. In the end, everyone ends up scrambling to fill in the gaps.

Fuzzy Goals are an example of unclear prioritization. When people don't know what matters most, they may end up working on unimportant projects that are misaligned with the team's most urgent and important jobs. They might be working hard, but it's the equivalent of running in the wrong direction.

Fuzzy Guidelines are when the boundaries, criteria, and constraints are not well-defined. They may lead people to spend time on unimportant features or inappropriate work. When it's finally clarified (usually when the hard-working employee presents the team with the fruits of their labours, only to hear: "That's not at all what we wanted..." from the mystified boss), the employee is understandably discouraged.

One common feature of fuzzy expectations is that the hassle usually becomes apparent only *after* the work is done. Miscommunications are a good (and annoying) example of this.

The funny (and unfortunate) thing about miscommunication is that it generally happens only when both people feel confident that there has been no miscommunication at all. Both parties feel the communication has been perfectly *clear*, so they don't see any confusion that needs to be addressed.

But, if expectations are consistently fuzzy, there is another hassle that will emerge over time: micromanaging.

Many people believe that micromanaging is all about power and control. Sometimes it certainly is.[74] But I personally think micromanaging is often a symptom of a deeper problem: low trust.

Think about it: Fuzzy expectations lead bosses to feel uncertain and untrusting. That, in turn, leads to micromanagement. Yes, they are trying to regain control, but not for the sake of feeling powerful - they are maybe just trying to ensure good results. And people certainly can't have much faith in achieving an outcome if that outcome wasn't clearly communicated in the first place.

While not all trust issues will be fixed with clearer expectations,[75] clearer expectations will *increase* trust on the team while also reducing the need for continual oversight and bothersome micromanagement.

Hassle #3: Pointless Stuff

When you ask employees what gets their goat, there is a third category of "hassle" that many people seem to mention: pointless stuff.

There is a strange paradox here: There are almost always *reasons* for this "pointless" stuff. Perhaps there is some policy that says it must be done. Perhaps a boring report is nevertheless part of a job description and could be used, at least in theory, to help higher-ups make decisions. Perhaps the

---

[74] More on this in Habit 6 - Bully Bossing.

[75] Another friendly reminder to make an appointment with that therapist...

"busywork" that's been assigned is merely to give the appearance that people on the team are already busy. Perhaps the meeting was switched from "conveniently online" to "inconveniently in-person" because the leadership wanted to emphasize team collaboration and camaraderie.

All those things *are* reasons. And sometimes they're very *good* reasons. But what employees seem to feel is that the reasons for this "pointless stuff" are not *compelling*.

In other words, employees describe stuff as "pointless" when they *don't know* the reasons for it, or when they *aren't convinced* by the reasons. Both these cases should prove useful for the aspiring "less-terrible" boss.

A boss obviously needs well-thought-out plans, but you also must *communicate* those plans. If you don't articulate the "why" behind the action you want people to take, it's very likely some of the folks on your team will think it's nothing more than a big hassle.

Complaints & Confessions

"I had this boss who made us drive out to the company office on the outskirts of the city for these little 45-minute meetings with him. It was like, an hour from where the team actually worked, so these meetings totally killed the whole morning or the whole afternoon. We could have *easily* done them virtually. I totally think it was a weird test of loyalty - like we'd have to show up and kiss the ring."

"My employee asked me once, 'How important is it to you that I attend this quarterly meeting in person?' I was a bit shocked. We were mostly remote, and I thought the team *loved* these meetings. I privately asked a colleague if they were concerned about this, and they responded, 'well... what exactly are we doing at the meeting? You haven't really told us.' I realized I hadn't communicated anything other than 'save the date', so I couldn't really blame my team for questioning whether it was a good use of their time. I felt like a bit of an idiot."

"I worked at this city office in the early 2000's, and we still had the big Cathode Ray Tube Monitors. Every afternoon in the spring and fall, the sun would shine in the window, which was nice, except that it would reflect off the computer screens. It literally made it *impossible* to see the screen. We put in requests for screen glare reducers. We put in requests for window blinds. We put in requests to rearrange the office desks. *None* of it ever happened. Our supervisor was a year from retirement and basically had one foot out the door. So for about an hour *every day* for a few months of the year, when the sun was shining just right, there were 6 of us who just couldn't do any work on our computers. Well... I guess one person made a makeshift sunshade out of an old cardboard box and worked like he was in a little cave, but the rest of us just took our coffee breaks when it was sunny. Total waste of time."

"I'm a graphic designer, and my manager would send me off to work on a project. I'd check in and show him my work-in-progress, and he'd basically tell me it was all wrong and that I should start over. I guess he didn't know what he wanted, but he knew what I did wasn't it. So that was frustrating. So I'd try to ask questions upfront, but then I wouldn't get any reply by email, and he was too busy for meetings. It basically just meant that I needed to re-do all the projects two or three times, and just learn to see my first drafts as him working out what he actually wanted."

Techniques to be Less Terrible

De-hassle-a-thons

Efficiency is always important, but it's rarely urgent. As a boss, you can help give your team permission to identify and dismantle the hassles that hold them back.

Consider scheduling a special working session: A De-hassle-a-thon.

Just like a "hack-a-thon", where teams work to make something useful under a tight deadline, a de-hassle-a-thon is meant as a working session to fix the stuff that's annoying them on a day-to-day basis.[76]

Notice a language choice: It's a *working session* - not a *meeting*. Why? Meetings feel like a hassle!

---

[76] For those familiar with Lean philosophy, what I'm suggesting is similar to a Kaizen event focused on hassles.

How long should the session be? Depends on what you think your team can handle. If your team is already overloaded with meetings, you might want to keep it short. Maybe start with an hour? But 90 minutes or a half-day might be more beneficial.[77]

Before the ~~meeting~~ working session, you might want to casually ask people what hassles they're dealing with. You might be able to make a list on your own based on their ongoing complaints.

Ideally, you'd facilitate this meeting to be biased towards *action*. We want people to identify and *fix* the hassles in-the-moment, not just talk about them. In reality, of course, some hassles will take longer to dismantle than others. You'll likely end up with a new project list of hassles to handle.

One manufacturing company I visited had made this part of their culture; *every day* started with 30 minutes of "efficiency time". People had *dedicated time* to fix the stuff that bugged them.

It's worth mentioning that some hassles that the team identifies may be unavoidable. Perhaps important policies or procedures will trump employee convenience, for instance. In these cases, you'll need to be an expert facilitator. Hear people out. Empathize. Don't get too defensive, but carefully explain the trade-offs and the reasoning. If the hassle has a bigger purpose and

---

[77] If they love it, they might want to do it again. That's the goal! But it's probably wise to keep it feeling like a "special event" rather than a "standing obligation".

employees start to buy in, it won't be perceived so negatively.

And don't forget to ask questions and treat it like a collaborative problem-solving exercise. It's not a complaining-session - it's a chance to get their ideas and focus their efforts to make stuff better!

The Definition of Done

To combat the hassle of fuzzy expectations, we need *very clear* expectations.

In any job, there are certain "must haves" and certain "would be nice's". Problems arise when people are unclear about which is which.

The Agile project management philosophy has a helpful concept: the Definition of Done. DoD, for short.

At a high-level, the definition of done is the set of criteria that determine when you can cross the thing off the list.

The specific model that my team and I have been using comes from Dan Martell.[78] Here's how he defines tasks and projects on his lists:

- Facts: What is true at the end of this? What are the metrics?
- Feelings: How do we need to feel at the completion of this project?
- Functionality: What does this need to enable others to do?

---

[78] Dan Martell wrote: Buy Back Your Time, which is a very nice collection of tools for busy entrepreneurs. But the tools work for teams too!

In my experience, writing these things down forces me to take a few minutes to think through the outcome I'm looking for. It can feel a bit pedantic, but it's worth it. The times when my teammates haven't delivered are the times when *I* was not clear in my definition of what needed to happen.

Clarify the Task Owner

Another tool to combat fuzzy expectations is to build the habit of clarifying the task owner.

We've all experienced the paralysis that comes from being unsure of who's supposed to do what. Failing to define team expectations might result in missed deadlines or doubling up on work.

While it's quite common for more than one person to contribute to a project, it's very helpful to have a *singular* point-person who is accountable for the outcome. Most people really do want to do a good job, but sometimes they're just not sure if a task is on their plate or on someone else's.

We ask this sort of question:

"If this doesn't get done, and we're looking around the room in a few months, who would we hypothetically point the finger at for dropping the ball?" [79]

Clarifying who's ultimately responsible for a thing saves everybody time and energy. Why?

---

[79] I recognize that "Finger Pointing" is part of an upcoming bad habit. As you'll read in Habit 4, I'm not suggesting you actually point the finger and *blame* people when things go wrong; I'm merely suggesting you use the question to clarify accountability and roles upfront.

1. Upfront clarity prevents the wasted effort that goes into figuring it out later (after the problems have emerged).
2. It gives the other people permission to focus elsewhere. Instead of worrying about every detail of every project, people can focus on the stuff for which *they* are responsible.
3. It helps get *you* out of the bottleneck role.

By default, the boss is probably viewed as the task owner. Everyone will assume that *you* are keeping tabs on how things are progressing. They'll think *you* are the person to ask when they have issues. But it's likely you're already overloaded. People are probably waiting on you, and you're probably making mistakes. Sometimes, *you* are the hassle.

But it's not just you. When *anyone* is overloaded, they drop the balls and create ripple effects of annoyance for everyone else. So, clarify the task owner and make sure the accountability is distributed across your team. It's empowering *and* hassle-reducing.

The "Next Action" Go-Round

Here's a simple process that will likely head-off many potential misunderstandings: End your meetings by going around the circle and having everyone state what they believe to be their "next action" (or actions) on the particular project.[80]

---

[80] David Allen's "Next Action Thinking" is an exceptionally useful tool. Go read Getting Things Done.

After some practice, it usually takes just 2-3 minutes to go around the group. The first few times, it could take 5-10 minutes or even more. This happens because at first, people will feel compelled to share *more* than their "next action". Over time, you can demonstrate that you're really only looking for a sentence. Maybe even just a few words - so long as they're the *right* sort of words.

Next actions always include a verb. Don't let people get away with just saying something like "contract" - it needs a verb to be clear and actionable. It should sound something like one of these:

- "I'm going to email so-and-so."
- "I'm going to draft up the contract."
- "Phone the supplier."

Even if it takes several minutes, this is time well-spent! Invariably, some people will realize there is confusion.

For example, it's common to realize someone was *not* crystal clear on what was expected, or it may emerge that two people believe they are in charge of the same task. Better to figure it out now and save everyone the hassle later on.

Get the Right Tools for the Job

Have a constant eye out for better tools.[81] As I mentioned before, people who work in the trades really understand the value of good quality tools.

---

[81] There is probably a better analogy when it comes to tools. Keeping an "eye out" sounds like someone forgot to wear their safety glasses.

I heard someone say: "I'm cheap - that's why I buy expensive tools. The tools need to work, and I only want to buy them once."

If you get the sense that people are using shoddy tools, advocate for getting them better ones. When people are less frustrated, they'll perform better, work more efficiently, and the whole culture will improve.

The $50 Magic Pill

Before my wife and I got married, a couples therapist gave us some financial advice: "Decide on an amount of money that either of you can spend, guilt-free, without consulting the other person."

It turns out this idea exists in the business world too: budgets! Budgets work because someone decided that it wasn't worth the hassle of reviewing every minor expenditure. Instead, the leadership team defines some rough allocation, defines some rough accountability mechanism, and then empowers their people to go do good work!

There's a specific, small-scale version of a budget that can be used to help de-hassle people: The $50 Magic Pill.[82]

Here's how it works: Give your team permission to spend up to $50, guilt-free, to solve a problem.

---

[82] With credit to Dan Martell for this catchy name.

Conditions? Sure... 1. Tell the boss that you spent it during your next meeting. 2. Explain what you spent it on.

Hesitant to spend the cash? Think about it this way: Your people's *time* costs money. Hassles and trivial problems can easily eat up *hours* of otherwise-productive time. If tasks are repetitive in nature (which many hassles tend to be), the effect compounds. So if someone can solve an annoying problem by spending some trivial amount of money, it's money well-spent!

Already have an official purchasing process on your team? Be honest. The hassle of going through some lengthy procurement process to spend 50 bucks is likely so discouraging that most people just won't bother. You need to make an informal policy! Of course, you can adjust the $50 amount to anything you feel comfortable with. For highly-paid professionals, their time alone might be worth several hundred dollars per hour.

Money can't solve all problems, but it can solve a lot of them! The $50 Magic Pill *saves* money, and giving people a fast way to de-hassle their lives saves everyone's sanity at the same time.

Final Words on Habit 3

A hassle-making boss shows up as someone who doesn't seem to care about the experience of their employees.

A highly defective hassle maker will create needless frustrations. Despite the ongoing wasted time and energy, they won't bother advocating for better tools. They're content to let fuzzy expectations stand without clarification. They may call needless meetings or invent pointless procedures that throttle down the team's performance.

Meanwhile, the aspiring less-terrible boss will actively make life easier for their employees. They'll ensure the team has access to functional tools. They'll get ahead of the confusion that comes from lack of clarity. They'll help people *avoid* pointless, annoying tasks.

Don't be a highly defective boss. De-hassle people to keep them happy and productive.

Don't be a hassle maker.

Reflect & Review

The relevant questions for Habit 3 - Hassle Making - were 7, 8, and 9:

7. I proactively identify and remove obstacles that frustrate my team.
8. I always set clear expectations and make sure my team has the tools they need for success.
9. I actively try to reduce the number of meetings and avoid micromanaging, even if I'm not sure what people are working on.

Habit 4
Credit Stealing & Finger Pointing

In almost every cartoon I watched as a kid, there was a big meanie of a villain who had some crony sidekick.

That poor sidekick was often sent away to do the villain's dirty work, but he'd *rarely* receive any praise or acknowledgement for a job well done. In fact, when the sidekick returned having carried out the plans, that big meanie of a villain would proclaim his *own* greatness in a longwinded rant about how smart he was to have hatched such a plan in the first place.

And by the end of the episode, when the villain's plans were inevitably foiled by the cunning hero, that big meanie of a villain would turn and *blame* the sidekick.

The ridiculous, self-centred, and insecure nature of the villain was written to be so blatantly obvious that even six-year-olds knew what was going on: The villain was the *real* fool. He stole the credit for the sidekick's work, and then pointed the finger when things went wrong.

Unfortunately for everyone, this pattern isn't confined to cartoons.

There seems to be a specific type of boss that mirrors our meanie villains. Insecurity lies at the root of both.

If you're insecure, you're probably looking to build yourself up. Fair enough. But there are healthier and unhealthier ways to do that, and this chapter deals with two of the less-healthy ways: Credit Stealing and Finger Pointing.

Credit Stealing

Let's go back to the boss' main job: Empower your team to do great stuff.

It turns out that people like to be recognized for their contributions and accomplishments. In fact, they *really* like it. More frequent recognition has been associated with all kinds of good outcomes: higher productivity, lower absenteeism, and even lower incidence of safety accidents.[83]

So people are out there, doing their good work, and if you're the boss, you just need to tell them that you see the good work they're doing! Give them the credit!

Unfortunately, some bosses end up *taking* the credit when things go well. Perhaps they want to look good in the eyes of *their* boss. Maybe they reason that they're the boss and it was their plan and leadership that made it possible. Maybe they actually feel so insecure and imposter-ish that they're trying to impress the people they're supposedly leading.

---

[83] Check out the Gallup & Workhuman report - The Human-Centered Workplace: Building Organizational Cultures that Thrive.

Alas, whatever the reasoning, nobody likes a credit stealer.

These insecure credit-stealing bosses would do well to realize that the best way to make themselves look better is to *give away* the credit. Or at the very least, *share* it.

If your team is achieving, *you* will look good. Onlookers will praise your effectiveness as a manager. The results will speak for themselves.

If you want your team members to achieve more (and like you more...), don't try to show everyone how great *you* are - tell them how great *they* are!

Credit-stealing Coaches? Rarely.

Need more convincing? Try imagining the coach of a pro sports team. In all those commercial-break or post-game interviews with professional-level coaches, have you *ever* seen a coach try to take credit for his players' successes?

"That last minute choice to pull the goalie - that was my call, and obviously it worked out really well. I called the time out, and I could have sent anyone onto the ice, but I chose our star player, and obviously my choice was great. I'd drilled those guys hard on that play during practice and I'm glad I did, because I won our team the game."

It's absurd to imagine. Even *bad* professional coaches don't talk like that. Need a shortcut? Count the I's and my's in that statement. Credit stealers hoard the glory.

Sadly, in the office context, it doesn't sound quite so unusual:

"I made the choice to swap out the project team as the deadline was approaching - they were behind schedule, so I pulled some strings and got our best people on the task. In the end, I caught three errors in the draft contract, but I managed to seal the deal and get it delivered."

Competent coaches give the team the credit:

"We knew we were down to the wire, so we took the time-out - obviously those are the times you rely on your star players. Our goalie was sharp the whole game and kept us in it. The guys had drilled these plays all year, but it's never easy when the pressure's on. We had three guys lined up ready to take the shot knowing they might get the chance, and the whole line had to work their tails off, but they managed to move the puck around enough to find an opening for a quick shot. Huge win for the team! They never stopped digging, and I'm so proud of them."

Want the office version?

"We knew we were behind, and the whole project team was already working overtime. We owe a big thanks to my colleague - he was a real team player and was able to lend us some reinforcements. I'm so proud of the whole team - everyone busted their butts to deliver this thing on time... all I did was review the final contract."

The people who understand sports know that coaches matter a lot. And in the world of work, people know that bosses matter a lot. Spread the love around; you don't have to hoard the credit.

Finger Pointing

When things are going well, defective bosses are prone to credit stealing. When things are *not* going well, those same folks are prone to finger pointing.

There's a saying: "Remember that when you point a finger at someone else, there are three pointing back at you."

The saying is supposed to remind you that blame and judgment are often a projection of one's *own* shortcomings. In psychoanalysis, the technical term is "projective identification." Essentially, we assign the feelings we don't like about ourselves onto someone else. This is merely supporting evidence that those who consistently judge others are usually deeply unhappy and critical of themselves.

Psychoanalysis aside, the issue at hand[84] is that finger pointing does very little to solve problems or help the team do good work.

An effective manager definitely needs to hold people accountable, but there's a big difference between seeking accountability and playing "the blame game".

Accountability is about ensuring everyone is clear on who is responsible for what. We want to be able to anticipate problems and address them efficiently. When things get off course, it's probably wise to clarify what went wrong, figure out which ball was dropped, and decide how to fix the issue. But it's also wise to stay focused primarily on productivity and teamwork.

---

[84] Hah!

Finger pointing, on the other hand,[85] is about scapegoating and judgment. While police might be concerned with finding the criminals, professional settings are different: Our intention should always be to solve the problem rather than merely find the perpetrator.

Focusing on blame easily strays into the territory of shaming, belittling, or punishing. It breeds fear, insecurity, and unhappiness. Blaming also tends to lead to defensiveness and *more* blaming, and soon enough, you have zero accountability and a toxic workplace.

When Things Don't Go Well

Any boss can easily imagine themselves to be doing an awesome job when things are going smoothly. The true test comes when things *don't* go according to plan.

Suppose someone misses a deadline. What should a boss do?

Certainly the employee needs to be held accountable. Missed deadlines have real consequences - frustrated teammates, slower project progression, and perhaps even lost business. But *how* should one address the issue?

Bosses have options. Here's a short, non-exhaustive list:

- Do nothing.
- Review the technicalities.

---

[85] Hah again!

- Ask for the employee's reasons.
- Re-explain the importance of the deadlines.
- Yell.
- Berate the individual.

Some of these are obviously better than others.

Likely, the boss *shouldn't* do nothing. Letting the incident slide could normalize the careless behaviour.

But once a boss has decided to do *something*, the details matter a lot. A boss might feel angry, but they should probably take a breath before they start their rampage.[86]

When a boss is quick to blame, anger, and point the finger, that boss is doing everyone a disservice: It's a disservice to the *employee* because it's causing needless pain and shame; it's a disservice to the *company* because assigning blame doesn't actually solve any problems; and it's a disservice to the *boss themself* because alienating employees and failing to solve a problem is a less-than-optimal use of time and energy.

Now you might be thinking, "But if the person who missed the deadline doesn't get in trouble, how will they know that what they did was unacceptable?"

This is actually the justification for most forms of punishment: If I can make you feel badly, then you will learn a lesson about what type of behaviour is acceptable. Sounds logical, right?

---

[86] In fact, they should probably take *many* breaths - enough breaths that they *don't* start the rampage.

Except it doesn't work. The research on punishment shows that making someone feel pain doesn't change behavior in the long-term.[87] This applies whether the pain be physical pain, social isolation (like a school suspension), or even shame and embarrassment (like by publicly humiliating someone for their errors).

Generally, people *want* to do well. When they don't, it's because they are lacking the skills essential for success. Since punishment doesn't teach a skill, it's unlikely to create better results.

An effective boss will focus on helping the team solve problems. That means they need to identify the weak spots and then coach people to do better.

Merely pointing the finger doesn't help get the team across the finish line.

Complaints & Confessions

"Years ago I worked for a municipality, and my boss asked for some data. My colleague put some rough ideas together, and I forwarded it on to my boss. She wrote back to me and was hyper-critical of the info we had sent, so that was annoying. But then,

---

[87] Check out Michael Karson's Psychology Today's article as a starting point. People (and rats) will try to avoid the *source of punishment*, but they won't really try to change the *behaviour that caused the punishment*. In other words, they'll avoid *you*, but they won't do things differently until you've taught them an alternative (more desirable) behaviour.

my boss copied the info word for word and packaged it up into a report for council. She presented it as if she herself had written it. She was totally two-faced - criticizing us but then using (stealing) the information without citing my colleague at all. I was so angry. It wasn't even *my* work, but my colleague should have got the credit."

"My boss was big on shaming and blaming. Whenever anything went wrong, she'd call a meeting and berate the culprit in front of everyone. The problem was that before long, everyone started hiding difficulties from her. Whenever she asked how things were going, everyone would claim they were going *perfectly* even when there were big problems. Soon, she had no idea what was going on in her own company; she'd only see problems when they'd become too big to hide, and certainly too big to fix."

"I had this one boss years ago who would constantly claim other peoples' ideas as his own. I don't think he realized he was doing it... like, I actually think it was sort of pathological. He couldn't *hear* the idea when it came from someone else. Someone would say the idea, he'd ignore it or shoot it down, and then say the same thing like it was brand new. And the whole team knew about this annoying quirk, too. Nobody *liked* it, but to get anything done, we had to devise these elaborate plans to plant ideas in the boss' head so he'd think they were *his* ideas."

"I worked for a really tough boss early on. She was super-perfectionist, and when things got missed or mistakes got made, she'd launch into these rants about how this person needed to do better or that person should have realized. But there was a strange thing: In her angry and blaming conversations *with* me, she'd never talk *about* me - it would always be about someone else. I suppose that spared my feelings a little bit in the moment, but mostly it just made me feel awkward. And I know she'd talk about me in her angry rants with *other* colleagues. How do I know? My colleagues told me! She was the same with everybody."

Techniques to Be Less Terrible

Share Your Philosophy of Leadership

The underlying philosophy here is simple: You look good when your team looks good.

Do *not* present yourself as the hero of your own story who must continually save the day and clean up the radioactive fallout from the nitwits who work for you.

Instead, *share* the credit with your team. Give accolades where they are deserved. Don't worry - you can still take responsibility for your role!

If you're worried *you* won't get fair recognition from *your* boss, you might try expressing your philosophy of leadership. It might sound something like: "My main job is to make sure my team is working well together and delivering results, and I'm really proud of their work. What do you think? Do you see things that I could be doing that would help with retention or performance?"

By being transparent and clear about how you view your role as a team leader, you might help *your* boss see things your way. And asking for their input gives your boss the chance to share their philosophy with you.

Sharing the credit means just that: sharing! And that includes some for you. You don't have to be so bashful that you deflect any compliment or praise that comes your way.

Systematize the Recognition

Even bosses who don't *intentionally* steal the credit might still miss opportunities to shine the spotlight on people's contributions.

Make yourself a plan where you recognize people *regularly*. It's probably wise to do something annually, but you should ideally plan things more frequently - quarterly and/or weekly.

Apparently only 1 in 4 people "Strongly Agree" with the phrase: "I've received recognition or praise for my good work within the last 7 days."[88] 1 in 4?! That's it?! Doesn't that feel abysmal? It did to me.

Except then I realized that a week goes by pretty quickly... And as I thought about it more, I realized that I might not even *talk* with some people every week. I think I'd beat the 1-in-4 stat, but I'm not where I *should* be. So, I'm working at

---

[88] That's from the Gallup & Workhuman report about organizational culture. The punchline is that recognition really matters.

it. And it's not that I'm "trying harder", it's that I'm consciously creating systems and "cues" to say genuine, nice things about the people on my team and the work they do.

Whether you have a standing weekly agenda item, or you make a commitment to end every 1-on-1 conversation with a "thank you" or a "way to go", *systems* will help you share those nice thoughts that are (probably[89]) already in your head.

Get Good at Coaching

A coach does not jump onto the basketball court during the final quarter or lace up her skates between periods. Coaches don't do the work *for* the players; they help the players be better.

Be like an excellent professional coach: It's your job to help people be better than they could be without you.

Bad coaches may point fingers and berate their players, but you can do better than that.

The Coaching Habit is a bestselling book by Michael Bungay-Stanier, and the big concept is that your curiosity is an undervalued resource. By asking more questions (as opposed to giving more answers), you position yourself as a useful resource, but not as a sole guru.[90]

This coaching approach empowers your people to find their own solutions. It eases the burden on

---

[89] ...hopefully?

[90] There's more coming on specific feedback techniques in the next chapter: Feedback Fumbling.

you. And it also makes it really easy to share the credit, because they're finding their own way.

And when things don't go well, you get to ask lots of questions. Rather than pointing the finger and making people feel worse than they do already, you'll help people identify missteps and find solutions on their own!

Start by Taking Responsibility

When things don't go well, start your conversations by taking responsibility for your part in things.

When you lead by example, two good things happen.

1. You increase the odds that other people will take responsibility for their parts; they'll be less likely to get defensive.
2. You create a culture where everyone admits errors more readily.

You don't have to take responsibility for everything, but by demonstrating that *you* are comfortable accepting some portion of the responsibility, you make it safer for everyone else to do so too.

Focus on "What now?"

To avoid blaming, keep your mental antenna tuned to the question: "What now?"

Obviously questions of *who* dropped which balls and *why* are important. It's usually helpful to know what went wrong so we don't make the same mistakes again. But those questions should always be asked in service of the more important question: "What should we do now?"

It's very easy for people to take things personally, (and this "What now?" philosophy is apparently uncommon,) so you'll need to emphasize that as a boss, *you* aren't going to focus on *who* made the mistakes. You can be explicit with people about what matters most: doing better next time.

People don't like messing up; they don't need to be chastised. People need to feel supported through their errors.

Final Words on Habit 4

Insecurity is often the root cause of people trying to hoard credit and avoid responsibility.

Everyone wants to feel recognized for their efforts and achievements, and they want to feel supported in their mistakes. Being a blame-y finger pointer never solves problems or gets the best from your team.

A highly defective finger pointer sees mistakes as a personality problem. They will spend time blaming, judging, and generally making others feel worse so they don't have to take responsibility for their *own* failures as a manager and project coordinator. Meanwhile, when things go well, these defective credit stealers are quick to claim all the glory for themselves.

The aspiring less-terrible boss employs a strategy of empowering and supporting their staff. They generously share the credit for successes. When things go awry, they model great communication, they shoulder responsibility for the failures, and they help people solve problems without making things personal.

Don't be a highly defective boss. Share the credit when things go well. Take responsibility when things don't.

Don't be a credit stealer, and don't be a finger pointer.

Reflect & Review

The relevant assessment questions for Habit 4 - Credit Stealing & Finger Pointing - were 10, 11, and 12:

10. I intentionally give public recognition and credit - especially to the folks who work behind the scenes.

11. When things don't go according to plan, I step up and take responsibility and I don't shift the blame; it might have been someone else's mistake, but I'm the leader.

12. My team isn't afraid to bring up mistakes; when someone drops the ball, they know I'll help fix the issue without causing more tension.

Habit 5
Feedback Fumbling

How many of us have had a satisfying and fulfilling performance review? (Cue the crickets...)

Performance reviews are often dreaded events. One Human Resources professional I know actually calls them "The Annual Slap-in-the-Face".[91]

Performance reviews may be viewed as an irritant. ("I don't have time for this.")

To some, they are scary. ("I have no idea how I'm doing, and I'm probably going to get scolded.")

To others, they are just plain pointless. ("My boss doesn't really pay attention to me and my goals anyway.")

This is a real shame, because without feedback, we're unlikely to experience growth.

That's not to say that feedback needs to come in the form of a formal performance review. In fact, the best feedback often comes through the most informal of conversations. But without *some* form of feedback, individuals stagnate and organizations struggle to keep people on track.

---

[91] Just to be clear, she didn't use this term proudly. She is working on changing the culture in her organization so feedback and performance reviews do *not* feel like an annual slap-in-the-face.

Most employees (and most *people*) really do *want* to grow and improve, so feedback should be an easy sell. A boss who's good at it should be able to develop better employees *and* retain them better. Giving effective feedback may be one of the most useful skills a boss can possess. Even so, the art of giving feedback is under-appreciated.

And of course, we can see things from the other side of the table. While managers face the challenge of *giving* good feedback, *everybody* faces the challenge of receiving it. And frankly, this can seem even harder.

How to Fumble Feedback

Let's say there are three basic ways to be "bad" at feedback - to fumble it, if you will.

The first way is to not provide feedback at all.

The second way to fumble is to give feedback, but do it *badly*.

The third way is to be bad at *receiving* feedback.

Simple, right? Except it isn't. It's hard, and many-a-boss have been resented for their bobbles.

The "No Feedback" Fumble

Not giving feedback at all - the "No Feedback" fumble - is perhaps the most obvious way to drop the ball.[92]

---

[92] Hah!

Why do some bosses resist giving useful and constructive commentary to their teammates? There are probably a variety of reasons. You can decide which one feels closest for you.

Some bosses may actually think it's *not important* to give feedback. After all, they're busy, and they reason that maybe people should be good at their jobs without "hand-holding".[93]

Some bosses might exist in such a competitive culture that sabotage and subterfuge are more common than helpful hints and honest collaboration.

Some bosses have a *fear of conflict* that stops them from speaking up or correcting mistakes.

Or maybe a defective boss is just too negligent to be able to provide constructive feedback for others. You know, maybe they just weren't paying attention.

But I'd bet the most *common* feedback-avoidance reason is that many people have people-pleaser tendencies; giving feedback can be uncomfortable.

If this is you, I'd invite you to dig into that a bit with a friend or (more ideally) a therapist. To play armchair psychologist for a moment:[94] It seems like a good bet to say that if you're a people-pleaser, probably someone criticized you a lot when you were

---

[93] Feedback is *not* hand-holding, but that's part of the mental error.

[94] Disclaimer: I'm totally not a psychologist. I'm not even writing this from an armchair. So if this resonates, get a second opinion from a real psychologist in a real armchair.

younger, and now you don't want to have any part in putting *that* bad experience onto others.[95]

That's noble. Caring, even! But what you've described[96] is *not* a reason to *not* give feedback - it's a reason not to be *mean and critical.*

In fact, your experience of being over-criticized actually makes you exceptionally well-qualified to give *sensitive* feedback. This is potentially a real strength.

That's not to say that offering feedback is always comfortable, because it isn't. Sometimes you may need to tell someone something they maybe don't want to hear. But again, that's not a reason not to do it.[97]

In fact, all of these reasons for not giving feedback fail to cut the mustard.

All these "no feedback" fumbling bosses are failing in their primary duty: empowering others to do a great job. Success as a manager depends upon one's ability to make *other* people awesome. And since individuals are better with feedback, and teams inevitably need guidance, *not* giving feedback is a losing strategy.

---

95 How'd we do?

96 Okay fine… what *I* described.

97 Also, check your assumption that the feedback you're about to give is 100% bad. It's probably not. And if it is, it shouldn't be.

The "Bad Feedback" Fumble

Even if a manager buys into the importance of feedback, there are still plenty of ways to mess it up.

Hopefully it's obvious, but we *don't* want our feedback to feel like the slap-in-the-face that so many people experience.

Lots has been written about this, but in my humble opinion, good feedback needs to have four key characteristics: conversational, actionable, timely, and sensitive. In this order, it makes a fun acronym: CATS. You could switch them to make it CAST. Or maybe ACTS. Or, if you like, I suppose you could choose any other number of permutations.[98] Anyway, I like CATS, so let's go with that. You can give me feedback on the acronym another time.

Let's dig into those CATS ideas.[99]

Conversational

Is there space for *everyone* to contribute?

There are really *two* practical ideas here.

Firstly, feedback that comes in the form of one-way communication is almost certain to be misinterpreted. So ditch those email memos and definitely don't lecture people. The most effective

---

[98] Well... not *any* other number of permutations. There are 4! = 4x3x2x1 = 24 potential arrangements of 4 objects, so you'd have to choose one of those. Which makes me wonder: How many ways can a math joke be arranged to seem pedantic?

[99] Or perhaps we should we say: "Let's get those CATS out of the bag."

conversations are just that: conversations! Why? A one-sided delivery technique fails to create the space for a discussion. It will likely leave an employee feeling disempowered.

Secondly, casual, day-to-day conversations are way less intimidating than formal performance reviews. If you can keep the feedback feeling light, your people are likely to be in a much better headspace to actually *hear* what you're trying to say.

As a bonus starting technique, consider asking for permission before jumping into it: "Can I offer some feedback?" Or maybe, "Is now a good time to share some feedback?" Getting some permission, especially if you have to share some challenging ideas, will help it avoid feeling like an ambush.

Actionable

Does your feedback lead to specific, constructive changes?

The goal of feedback is to help the employee grow into a strong contributor for the team. Too often, feedback seems irrelevant because the conversation doesn't lead to any clear behaviour changes. Without a constructive outcome, feedback conversations can stray into the territory of blame and judgement. As we saw with the bad habit of finger pointing, blame is discouraging and disempowering.

There are *many* specific techniques to guide feedback conversations toward actionable steps. I especially like "Start-Stop-Continue" and "Next-

Action Thinking", but any great boss should have a small arsenal of effective conversation tools.[100]

Timely

Are people getting feedback when it still feels relevant?

If there's an issue, you probably should bring it up as soon as you can, unless you have a good reason to delay. Bringing it up quickly gives you the best chance of getting good information from everyone, and it gives everyone the best opportunity to correct the issue, find a remedy, and adjust for next time.

Plus, sitting on feedback risks making everyone feel even worse. Just imagine how you'd feel if someone brought up an issue that happened three, six, or even eleven months ago, just after your last annual performance review. Your mental wheels would start turning to fill in the gaps: "*Have you been upset with me for this whole time? Why did you wait this long? Are you building a case against me to fire me? What else have you not told me?*"

Sensitive

Do you deliver in a way that lets everyone keep their dignity?

Feedback inherently involves sensitive conversations. We all want to feel proud of our contributions! In an ideal world, maybe we would all be reasonably self-assured people - confident

[100] Conveniently, we'll share a few tools in a few moments!

but not cocky, and we'd be experts at separating our professional performance from our sense of personal self-worth. In reality though, most of us need at least occasional reassurance.

When we are recognized for our contributions, we feel great and we try to do even better. But we sometimes need to hear information that does *not* make us feel proud. In these cases, the *way* someone delivers their feedback is doubly important. It's dejecting to be flat-out criticized.

A boss' comments can have a big effect on someone's confidence, drive, and even their happiness. The boss has a position of power, and for better or worse, their opinion matters. Bosses ought to be sensitive.

When you put all this together, feedback feels like a collaborative, constructive, and even creative, conversation. In fact, putting these things together makes each of them easier to do! It's easier to provide actionable feedback when it's timely. It's easier to give timely feedback (and in a sensitive way) when it feels conversational rather than overly formalized or uni-directional. It's all mutually reinforcing.

Great bosses are like great coaches: They help everyone on the team do better than they would on their own.[101]

But still, some people will rightfully point out that in sports, there are a lot of different models for

---

[101] You're likely noticing the coaching theme here. It's true! Boss-ing and coaching have lots of overlap.

successful coaches. Some of them yell and call people names. Some are vindictive. Some throw water bottles as they tantrum around the dressing room.[102]

So what happens when some "straight-shooter" boss believes that honest, formal feedback is the way to get great results? They may even try to throw a few positive nuggets your way, but mostly, they lay out the "facts" as they see them in your awkward once-a-year review: *"Here is where you are lacking. This thing happened months ago - it was a major issue for everyone on the team - and I expect better next time. Here's a few good things you did. Get back to it."*

Well, most people would leave that sort of "conversation" feeling unappreciated, discouraged, and resentful.

That straight-shooter boss is clearly not concerned about how their feedback makes employees feel. They might not possess the emotional intelligence to consider the impact of untimely criticism. They may feel that the employee's feelings are the employee's problem. *"Performance is what matters,"* they might proclaim! Sadly, this highly defective boss fails to realize that an employee's feelings and motivation are *linked* to performance!

An effective manager will be an expert in delivering constructive feedback that addresses awkward issues with kindness and supportive intent. When it's delivered well, difficult conversations about

---

[102] At least, *one* of my hockey coaches did this. My 10-year-old self probably looked up to that guy, but in retrospect, we weren't a very good team, and he almost certainly was not a great coach.

errors and changes can feel motivating! Even the most performance-driven boss ought to realize the benefit of CATS - conversational, actionable, timely, sensitive - feedback.

The "Can't Take Feedback" Fumble

There's a final way to drive your employees round the bend that relates to feedback, and that is to be bad at *receiving* feedback.

While bosses are often saddled with the official duty of offering feedback to their employees, they're certainly not the only ones with opinions. Employees *also* have observations and ideas about how to do things better. They have feedback for the boss!

But maybe the boss never asks the employees for feedback. That's a fumble.

Maybe the boss asks, but isn't really open to it and gets all defensive when employees share.

Or maybe they ask, seem open to it, but then fail to do anything differently.

All of these fumbles will cause frustration in your employees, and it'll be even worse if you're *also* bad at giving feedback; nobody likes a hypocrite or double standards.

The truth is that bosses benefit from feedback just as much (or more) than others, because they potentially influence more people. That means their positive traits have more benefits and their errors do more damage. But also, managers potentially deal with a broader range of people, so their jobs may be more challenging. Bosses would benefit from all the help they can get.

But the other truth[103] is that bosses are humans too,[104] so all the reasons that employees resist feedback apply just as readily to bosses.

We don't want to look foolish. We want our team to respect us. All that stuff about bits of your self-worth being bound up in your professional accomplishments - it all still applies. Let's face it: It won't feel too satisfying to tell your mom about your new promotion to "team lead" if everyone on the team thinks you're an incompetent jerk. Instead of risking being exposed to some hurtful truth, it almost always feels easier (at least in the moment) to avoid asking what people really think.

What else gets in the way of being open to feedback? Maybe you're overly tied to tradition. It's easy to fall into the *"this is the way we've always done it"* mentality. Change causes uncertainty, and that can be hard. But when we really examine our resistance, it's usually just our egos.

The good news is that the bar for bosses seems to be pretty low. It's so rare that bosses even *ask* for feedback (let alone acting on it) that, when you *do* do[105] it, your people might be so pleasantly surprised

---

[103] Okay, not *the* other truth... *an* other truth... but it's *the* other one I'm specifically mentioning in this section.

[104] And yes, some readers with terrible (inhuman) bosses may be questioning the validity of this *other* truth. Bear with me: "bosses are humans" is the *premise*, the *next* bit is what I'm claiming is the truth...

[105] Sorry. I couldn't avoid the do do.

they'll think you're a superstar. And, hey! Since you're so open to feedback, let me offer a little Yoda-esque feedback of my own: If feedback you can take, a superstar, you are indeed!

Complaints & Confessions

"I served as the chair of the board for a non-profit arts organization. Technically, the board of directors is responsible for hiring the Executive Director and the Artistic Director, which means we were also responsible for their performance reviews. But none of us really felt qualified to offer feedback - we were all volunteers and really only knew what the two staff were reporting to us. I defaulted to sharing some candid feedback, and I didn't do it well. In fact, one of them got so upset that I felt lucky they didn't quit. In other words, in trying to fulfill my 'supervisory duties', my feedback discouraged (and almost drove away) the person who was essentially the organization's most valuable contributor."

"My old boss was fine at listening to feedback - he'd ask for input all the time. But there was almost never any action... It was almost worse than if he'd have just never asked."

"I knew our management was bad at giving performance reviews because I literally had to debrief with colleagues after each of their sessions. They usually ended up crying because the boss had brought up some small thing that happened 8 months ago, but they brought it up like it was an enormous issue."

"I work in HR, so we're supposed to be good at this stuff, but every year we have issues. We've talked at length about giving better performance reviews, but managers just seem to default to their old habits. Honestly, we should probably just ditch the things. It feels like they're doing more harm than good."

"A boss once told me that I was being put on probation, but they tried to make it seem like it wasn't a big deal. But being put on probation *is* a big deal. I was blindsided. I knew she and I weren't always on the same page, but I had no idea that I was doing *that* badly. And she actually put a smiley-face sticker on the official letter that laid out why I wasn't cutting it. I guess she was trying to lessen the blow, but it felt totally tone-deaf."

Techniques to be Less Terrible

Default to Feedback About Yourself

If you want to create a culture where feedback is welcomed and sought-out, start by doing that yourself.

Any time you give feedback for someone else, start with asking if they have any feedback for you.

More Questions Than Statements

When we feel misunderstood or unheard, we reject any assessment of us as being out-of-touch.

Instead of starting with a list of things you want to say, try starting with a list of questions you want your employee to think about.

Questions generate answers. Statements often generate resistance.[106] Develop your coaching skills and use your curiosity to help people come to their own conclusions.

One simple feedback technique that's often overlooked is asking the employee how *they* feel about their performance. Here are a few questions that do this:

- *"What's one thing YOU think you did well?*
- *What's one thing YOU think you could do better?"*
- *"What skills would you like to work on during the next year, and how can I support you in that?"*
- *"What's one thing that could be changed about our team to make everything go more smoothly?"*[107]

Invite Collaborative Input

When you're doing a post-mortem on a big project, or even looking back on a random week of work, try making the feedback conversation more collaborative in nature. Again, do more asking than telling.

---

[106] ... err... don't you think?

[107] Note the inclusion of both task- and people-focused questions. Remember that Function Forgetting stuff?

A team performance review ought to feel more like a collective debrief and offer everyone a chance to speak their minds.

Whether you use open-ended questions or are trying to narrow in on a few specifics, invite others on the team to share their ideas. In all likelihood, they'll organically bring up most things *you* were going to say.

The Annual Review: More Career-Focused

Since there's a constant tractor-beam towards the day-to-day, it's more important to intentionally carve out time for longer-term career-related conversations.

While some may suggest ditching your "annual performance review", I'd suggest keeping a slot in your schedule for an "annual career check-in" with each of your people.[108]

Instead of looking back at specific projects, make the conversation about their skills and goals. Use that stuff as a starting point to talk about areas for growth, team needs, roles, and how to help them get where they want to go.

Reality-test Your Observations

Before you lose your cool, ask some questions to learn more.[109] Psychologists call this "reality-testing".

---

[108] Again... Re-read Habit 1 - Function Forgetting.

[109] And once again, you should try to *not* lose your cool at all, but this technique will help with that too.

We all make "observations", and those observations help form *our* version of reality, but the thing about our observations is that we almost never see the whole picture. Our brains fill in the gaps.

In other words, we make assumptions without realizing they are assumptions. This leaves us in dangerous territory. My colleague Brandon advises asking a specific question: "What am I missing?"[110]

For instance, I heard a success story of a boss who did this: He noticed someone was showing up five-minutes late for work almost every day. Instead of getting upset, he asked a mutual colleague if *they'd* noticed anything and if they had any insight into what might be going on.

Turns out, that late arriver regularly stayed fifteen minutes extra at the end of the day and usually worked through her lunch. As far as the colleague was concerned, there was no problem at all, and she advised strongly against even mentioning it, unless it was to recognize her outstanding commitment or officially offer a flexible schedule to help with childcare drop-offs.

By reality-testing, the boss saved himself from agitating a dedicated employee.

Make a habit of taking a pause and asking questions to validate your observations.

---

[110] Check out Brandon Love online: brandonlove.co - He uses magic to help leaders avoid embarrassing assumptions.

My Favourite Feedback Model

When it comes to giving and getting feedback, there are literally dozens of models. In my opinion, the best ones have some commonalities:

- There's more positive than negative.
- They're mostly forward-looking (rather than backward-looking).
- There's two-way input.

Here's the model I default to using:

- 3 Strengths
- 1 Area for Growth
- Ideas for how to *use* the strengths to achieve the growth

To highlight this with an example, suppose an employee is great with people and great at *doing* well-defined tasks, but you need them to be more proactive in *identifying* the action-items and *defining* the tasks. Your feedback notes might look like this:

- 3 Strengths:
    1. Build rapport quickly
    2. Ability to ask great questions
    3. Follow-through on assigned projects
- Area for Growth:
    - Identifying projects and action items from client meetings
- Ideas for How (using the strengths):
    - Try to finish meetings by asking questions to clarify what projects and action-items have emerged.

  - Trust you've got enough rapport to do it - you won't seem pushy by asking.
  - We know you're good at "getting things done" - so let's try thinking of a meeting as being "done" only after the next actions are identified and physically added to our list.

I didn't invent this model,[111] but what I especially like about it is that it's strengths-based. It doesn't ignore the need for change, but it feels empowering. And it's particularly effective in two-way conversations.

Here are a few *extra* tips if you are using this model with an employee in a 1-on-1.

- Both people will talk about both people.
  - That means you *and* the employee each prep reflections for *both* of you.
- Do your prep ahead of time.
  - I'd suggest writing it down.
- The conversation *order* is flexible, but by default, I choose this order:
  - We ease into it.
  - You talk about me.
  - I talk about me.
  - You talk about you.
  - I talk about you.

I love that I get to recognize the skills and unique contributions of my team while also learning

[111] It's possibly Brene Brown's? She has written a lot about giving great feedback.

more about their goals and their perceptions of their strengths. So far, at least the times when I've done it, it works well.

Final Thoughts on Habit 5

Feedback is hard because people's fragile egos get tied up with their performance.

Highly defective feedback fumblers will either avoid giving feedback, or they'll give feedback so insensitively that it might have been better if they'd said nothing at all. Meanwhile, these same bosses may outright reject any feedback pointed back in their direction.

The aspiring less-terrible boss knows feedback matters, and they learn to do it well. Instead of doling out critical comments that are likely to be poorly received, they get good at asking questions. After all, employees often *know* what they need to improve.

Rather than filling the role of a human compliance whip, a less-terrible boss can become a conversational partner in problem-solving. They also demonstrate their *own* willingness to receive feedback.

When staff see that a manager is taking feedback seriously, they feel both accountable and acknowledged - both important tenets of a healthy work environment. Best of all, good feedback will help managers unlock their team's best performance.

Don't be a highly defective boss. Build your skills in giving feedback that's conversational, actionable, timely, and sensitive.

Don't be a feedback fumbler.

Reflect & Review

The relevant assessment questions for Habit 5 - Feedback Fumbling - were 13, 14, and 15:

13. My employees consistently respond well to my coaching and feedback.

14. I regularly ask for feedback, my team shares their honest thoughts with me, and I make sure I act on their suggestions.

15. I give feedback - even critical comments - in a constructive and emotionally-sensitive way.

Habit 6
Bully Bossing

There is perhaps no stronger stereotype of the bad boss than the hard-headed bully.

Although it's easy to imagine the boss who barks orders at whoever is around, demands that people "shape up or ship out", and pompously belittles the work of others, this "meanness" is only one form of bullying.

Some of the most harmful and upsetting behaviour is quiet, underhanded, and more insidious. It's much harder to catch because it can be camouflaged as ordinary interaction. It's often *relational* in nature, rather than physical.

Let's put it in movie-terms. Back to the Future has Biff: He's a big, loud, dimwitted goon. But Mean Girls has Regina George: She's sly, manipulative, crafty, and socially-intelligent. Biff and Regina may have slightly different tactics, but they have a few things in common: They're power-hungry bullies who try to control people with fear.

The Feeling of Being Bullied

My wife Kathleen is a conflict coach and bullying expert,[112] so she's quite familiar with how

[112] Well… anti-bullying expert. You know what I mean.

these power dynamics show up and what gets in the way of dealing with them.

Lots of people don't like the word "bullying", so let's get that clarified.

If someone says something unintentionally offensive, we could say that's *rude.*

If someone says something *intentionally* offensive, we could say that's *mean.*

If someone is repeatedly mean, especially to the same person, we could say that's *bullying.*

Can you think of bosses that are repeatedly mean? Probably. They're bully bossing. The weird thing is, it's always easier to see bullying from the outside. It's much harder to recognize it when it's happening to you.

People often don't *realize* they're being bullied. Often, the feeling of being bullied first emerges as a sense of deep shame. Rather than thinking, "That's a bully," people often end up feeling something closer to: "There's something wrong with *me.*"

So, sometimes the easiest way to diagnose whether you have a bully boss is to look at how things feel in your workplace. In the spirit of this being habit six, here are six things to look for:

1. You come home from work emotionally exhausted and yearn for the weekend.
2. You approach going to work (or having meetings) with anxiety and dread.
3. You leave meetings feeling doubtful of your skills or achievements, even if you arrived feeling confident.

4. You feel confused by opaque decision-making or your boss' refusal of reasonable requests.
5. You feel discouraged or frustrated by blocked opportunities for promotion or training.
6. Your office or team has a high turn-over rate, and honestly, you're not that surprised.

Once you've taken stock of how you feel, try looking with objective eyes at your boss' actions. See how many of these next six things apply:

1. They gossip or humiliate people in front of others (or they allow others to do so).
2. They downplay emotional issues and question the experiences of others (gaslighting).
3. They frequently yell or make showy displays of aggression and disappointment.
4. They over-supervise and monitor your every move, failing to provide any trust or privacy.
5. They steal credit and claim others' ideas as their own.
6. They reject what seem like reasonable ideas as risky, reckless, or just plain stupid.

If this sounds familiar, you might want to seek out some help from HR, or even start looking for another job. Sadly, a bully boss is unlikely to change.[113]

---

[113] And if this stuff sounds like *you*... umm... just kidding! Bully bosses like you can *totally* change! Please, *do*! Read on, my friend! Here, take my lunch money!

The problem is that these bully bosses usually have deeply-held beliefs about what gets results: power tactics and fear.

Fear is an Energy Drain

When a boss uses fear to create motivation, staff end up devoting a lot of energy to *managing* the fear instead of using that energy to simply do their work.

Think of the last time a boss made a comment that made you feel threatened. Now recall how much time and energy you spent wrestling with how to respond.

You probably called your friend or debriefed the situation with your spouse. I've had times where I have literally spent tens of *hours* over several *weeks* trying to figure out how to navigate a tricky situation. Even when I was at work, my mind would often wander off-task and start noodling on how I might approach things when the opportunity arose.

Just think of how much more effectively I could have been using my time!

At worst, those tricky dynamics send people into mental health spirals. At best, that stuff is a huge distraction from the tasks on the list.

But Does Fear Get Results?

So, we acknowledge that leading with fear has some negative effects. But hey, the boss is simply demanding results, right?

Perhaps the *real* problem is that some people just aren't cut out for the job? Maybe this fear-mongering mentality actually helps the company do better?

Nope.

Not only is fear a time-waster and an energy-drain, but it also affects quality of work.

Think of how you felt right before a big test back in school. What feelings come to mind? If you're like most people, "stressed" is near the top of the feelings list.

One of the big criticisms of testing is that lots of people don't do their best work under this type of fear and pressure. Gentle pressure can be good, but not the "all is lost if I don't get this right!" level of pressure. Usually, that just freezes up someone's mind.[114]

Fear is known to shut down creative thinking; the fight, flight, freeze, or fawn response it creates gives people tunnel vision. Scared people miss potential opportunities and become blind to solutions that would seem obvious in a more relaxed, trusting environment.

So if your boss is instilling fear and high levels of stress, you're likely to show up at work feeling a lot like you did back in those younger, school days.

---

[114] There's actually a lot of nuance to this topic. Check out the 2025 research: "Does Stress Lead to Success?" Sometimes higher-stress ("arousal" in research-terms) can be helpful. Sports teams and surgeons (and probably others) do better if they're a bit riled up beforehand... but not *too* riled up.

- You'll be fearful of doing anything differently.
- You'll focus on blending in and avoid drawing attention to yourself.
- You'll stop thinking creatively.
- Free from any independent thinking, your work will become monotonous drudgery.

Sounds pretty terrible, eh?

A boss certainly needs to take work seriously, hold people accountable, and pay attention to results. But that doesn't mean a boss needs to lead with fear and power tactics. While a "tough guy" or "tough gal" boss may get short-term results from workers, these results are destined to remain short-lived. Why?

In the long run, the value of relationships in the workplace (and also probably in life…) far outweighs the value of any individual project.

On an individual level, people who feel bullied into submission will build up resentment and aren't likely to put forward their best efforts. Plus, for all the reasons we just mentioned, they'll perform *worse.*

On an institutional level, high resentment is linked with low trust. Progress slows down in a low-trust environment because everything has to be triple-checked and signed-off upon. Turnover rates skyrocket. Efficiency plummets as experienced team members walk away and new team members need training. The company will likely feel stagnant. The employees will feel stuck, discouraged, and disempowered.

In short: No - Leading with fear does *not* get better results.

Strong AND Kind

Some bosses are bully bosses because they think that being mean is the best way to get results; they are worried about being perceived as "lax", "apathetic", or "weak". These traits would *indeed* be concerning in a boss, but there is flawed thinking here.

We can gain some insight with a quick game of *opposites.* Let's play!

What's the opposite of "lax"?
I'd say "diligent". Or perhaps "strict".

What's the opposite of "apathetic"?
"Driven"? Perhaps "results-oriented"?

What's the opposite of "weak"?
Strong. That's an easy one.

Wasn't that a fun game?

Notice that the word "mean" is not the opposite of *any* of those worry words. *Mean* is the opposite of *kind.*

A boss who is diligent, strict, driven, results-oriented and strong can *also* be kind.

I know what you're thinking: It sounds like another 2x2 matrix! Strong-Weak on one axis, Mean-Kind on the other. It works!

But wait! We could add another dimension: Let's add Driven-Apathetic to make it a 2x2x2 cube with 8 possible regions. And we could keep going! Adding Lax-Diligent would make a four-dimensional

2x2x2x2 hypercube. Sixteen combinations - like the Myers-Briggs model.

And why stop there? Actually... *let's* stop there.[115]

Despite my enthusiasm for n-dimensional hypercubes, maybe a Venn diagram is a better visual for this idea. Let's bring this back to two categories: strong, and kind. (We'll lump those ideas of diligent and driven in with "strong".)

Kathleen (that lovely wife of mine), has figured out a nice way to say this:

The good thing about being "strong" is that people get their needs met. But when people are *only* "strong", it often feels like they're trying to power *over* people. They're using force to get their way.

The good thing about being "kind" is that you maintain relationships. But when people are *only* "kind", they power *under* others. They too-easily give in to others' demands and give up their own needs.

The key is to find the overlap in the Venn diagram! When people are both strong *and* kind, they

---

[115] We *should* stop there for at least two reasons: 1. Because I admit it's no-longer simple. And 2. Because my wife Kathleen says so, and she's the expert.

find power *with* others. They stand up for their interests, but they also maintain relationships.[116]

Everyone's "strong and kind" voice will sound unique. People express themselves differently, and it needs to feel authentic. It also may change with the context; the strong and kind voice you use with your colleagues may be different from the strong and kind voice you use at home or with your friends.

Kathleen has found that when people *do* find their strong and kind voice, their relationships improve. Notably, bullying relationships dissolve almost instantly because the bullies can no longer get the power they need.

Bullies themselves are often lacking conflict management skills. Part of Kathleen's work is helping them develop *healthier* strategies to resolve conflict. There is often trauma underneath the anger, but she has found that once people have the skills (including their strong and kind voices), they usually use them.

So I was probably being a bit pessimistic back a few pages ago when I said bullies were unlikely to change. Bullies *can* change, but probably not without some serious work.

If you have a bully boss, your best bet is to find your strong and kind voice.

---

[116] While Kathleen has really nailed the *wording*, I'll take the credit for the Venn Diagram visualization. She thinks my proclivity for math-y diagrams is a bit goofy. But she represents power-over, power-under, and power-with as cute little personified-pear cartoons: Prickly Pear, Petrified Pear, and Positive Pear... So who seems goofy now?

If *you're* of the mind that fear and power-tactics are working for you, work on adding more "kind" into your "strong". It'll probably work even better.

Complaints & Confessions

"There was one boss I had who was super-hard to work for. I never knew where I stood with him. I'd leave almost every meeting questioning myself: 'I *thought* I did a pretty good job on this, but now I'm not so sure.' It was like, instead of empowering people, he was constantly seeding doubt. I think he really created a sense of fear in people."

"My boss always needed to be in charge. She'd demand we do needless things as tests of loyalty. Soon enough, everyone dreaded her coming into the room. As soon as she entered, the whole mood would shift. As a result, she never saw her company operating authentically; she missed all the laughter and fun! She must have thought her company was full of nothing but timid, quiet, fearful people when really it was anything but."

"My boss was passive aggressive. She once unnecessarily cc'd a whole committee of colleagues, including *her* boss, on an email where she was critical of how I'd handled a proposal I worked on. I remember stewing for days about that... It was so manipulative. I was embarrassed, and I was angry, but it felt like she had the upper hand. If I wrote back to everyone, *I'd* look like the jerk who was arguing by email. I can't say for sure, but it felt like my reputation took a hit. I was happy to move on to another position when I had the chance."

"I used to work for a big tech company, and we went through a round of layoffs where hundreds of people were let go at the same time - mass email style. I know that layoffs are part of the gig in that world, but the boss was so *insensitive* about it all. The whole culture changed that day. How a leader acts when people are vulnerable says a lot. A job loss is a big deal, and a boss should be able to terminate someone's employment without taking away their dignity, you know?"

Techniques to be Less Terrible

Find Your Strong and Kind

Next time you're in a tricky situation, do a little work to explore what your personal strong and kind voice sounds like.[117]

A good way to do this is to take a few minutes to brainsprout[118] all the possible things you could say in a given situation. Basically, write down as many possibilities as you can come up with. Some of the ideas may be mean. Some may be totally

---

[117] This is an overview of Kathleen Hilchey's tried and tested process. Credit to her!

[118] This is a reference to the book I wrote with Brandon Love - Brainsprouting. Credit to ~~he and me~~ ~~him and I~~ us!

passive. Some might be super silly. It's all good! Get them all out onto paper.

Once you've got a big list, look back over it. Eliminate anything that's *only* kind or *only* strong. There'll often be one that jumps out at you - something that *feels* like an easy next step.[119]

The odd thing is that once you have found the right response, the original "tricky" situation might feel surprisingly *easy*. You might have just found one version of your strong and kind voice!

Of course, you don't need to reserve your strong and kind voice for tricky situations; use it all the time! Finding healthy power with the people around you communicates respect and builds trust.

Prioritize Relationships

In conflict, it's easy to feel a tension between two things: results and relationships.

We can easily see that the harder we fight, the more we risk damaging the relationship. We're not *trying* to be mean, but we also don't want to give up, so we often push harder and harder.

If you're using your strong and kind voice, you'll already be balancing results with relationships. But this tip takes it one step further.

I'm going to make an odd claim: Prioritizing the relationship obviously leads to a better relationship, but it *also* increases the chances of getting what you want.

---

[119] Look up Kathleen Hilchey online. She's got a free poster and video to help with this process.

You don't have to completely give up on your interests, but skewing your approach towards preserving relationships will work out better in the long run. Maintaining good rapport will help *every* future problem.

Empowerment Beats Control

I've tried to paint the picture that there are *kind* ways of holding people accountable and getting good results. Bully bosses tend towards micromanagement, and that's a big problem.

Progressive companies are learning that micromanagement not only stifles motivation, but it also *lowers* the quality of the product.

Think about it: One of the main benefits of a team is the presence of multiple perspectives and skillsets! But, a group's synergy and capacity for innovation is quashed if the individuals aren't free to contribute their own unique talents. Micromanagement and control tactics shut down those creative perspectives.

Obviously it can be hard to relinquish control and let go of the reins (or at least give them a little slack), but that doesn't mean it's a bad idea. Some bosses may think controlling every aspect of a project is the best way to ensure a top-quality result, but they are sorely mistaken. True leadership is about empowerment, not control.

The "How Can I Help?" Question

Since you're the boss, people are likely to come to you with their challenges. It's very easy to assume that everyone wants you to solve their problems.

My wife taught elementary school for a year, and she remembered the rant of a fifth-grade girl who taught *her* a great lesson.

The girl said, "You adults always want to jump in and solve things. Sometimes we don't want that! Why don't you start by asking if we want help."

Kathleen took it to heart, and ever since, she tries to start with that question. The version she uses (and the one I adopted for myself) sounds like this: "Do you want me to just listen, give you advice, or problem solve this together?"[120]

You build trust and rapport just by asking this question, and you build even more trust when you actually do what they ask.

Instead of disempowering people by bulldozing the conversations and pretending you know all the answers, ask people how they want you to help.

Get Some Therapy

After a few scattered footnote references about getting therapy, let's make this official: Get some therapy.[121]

---

[120] A friend told me he'd heard a slightly different version: "Do you need to be heard, helped, or hugged?" It's cute, right? But maybe don't ask it this way in the workplace.

[121] If you're highly resistant to this idea, I doubt this will change your mind. But I'm okay with that. By the way... How many psychologists does it take to change a light bulb? Give up? Just one, but the light bulb has to really *want* to change.

When you get angry, you're all charged up about something that's important to you. But nobody makes their best decisions when they're in that state of mind. Even when you're feeling really *good* - when you're super excited, for instance, you're probably not thinking too clearly either.[122]

You need to figure out what's going on inside *you.* It just so happens that therapists are people who can help with that. Just as doctors can help us understand various parts of our physical bodies, therapists can help us understand our emotions and relationships. Our minds are just as vulnerable to "illness" or "faults" as our bodies.[123]

There's still some societal stigma around seeing a therapist. When I was growing up, I don't think my family *discouraged* it, but it certainly wasn't promoted. Many people still (wrongfully) seem to think that if you're seeing a therapist, you must be "crazy". This is an outdated idea.

Therapists are trained to hold space for you to explore what's going on inside your head so you see things *more clearly.* And because they're

---

[122] Remember those times back in high school when you were so infatuated with that special someone that you made questionable choices about being late for class and/or sneaking out of the house to spend a few extra moments with them? No? My therapist assures me it's not just me.

[123] Actually, our minds are probably *more* vulnerable. I'm not saying we're all bound to have mental health issues, but I make logical errors and misinterpret others' intentions just about every day. Cognitive biases are literally built into our neurology. We can't escape it!

detached from your life, they can be honest with you in a way your friends and family can't be.

As kids, we all learned "lessons". Sometimes those lessons were explicit, but many more of the lessons were *implicit* - we learned them by observing how the world works. The problem is that many of the lessons were not very wise.[124] Some lessons were muddled with inconsistency.[125]

Therapists help us identify the rules and lessons we are subconsciously following. Once we see our mental patterns more clearly, we can decide if we want to change course or keep going.

In short, you'll be wiser if you're willing to challenge your own assumptions. Therapy isn't the only way to do that, but it'd certainly help.

Final Words on Habit 6

Despite what many of us learned on the schoolyard, fear and threats are not the only way to get what you want.

---

[124] Need an example? Most of us were raised to believe that "tattletales" are bad. Still believe it? Are you *sure*? Don't want people standing up for what's right? Disagree with alerting the folks in charge if you see something you can't handle on your own? Feel the same about whistleblowers?

[125] Parents and teachers drilled into us about our manners: "Say please and thank you!" Meanwhile, those silly adults yelled and humiliated the poor kids when they forgot. Some adults still beat their kids to teach them lessons. Do polite words really matter more than those adult actions?

Highly defective bully bosses think that power-tactics help the team perform better. They make showy displays of anger, gaslight their staff, and downplay the emotional trauma they are inflicting on the team. And apparently, they're either ignorant or apathetic about the immense costs of their bully-bossing approach: decreased productivity, high turnover, and the snuffing out of any semi-positive vibes.

Meanwhile, the aspiring less-terrible boss recognizes that they don't have to choose between being strong and being kind - they can be strong *and* kind. Being diligent and driven doesn't mean they need to be mean, and they *won't* be mean, because they understand the value of long-term relationships.

Maybe most importantly, these less-terrible bosses know how to recognize their own emotions. They figure out healthy ways to deal with their stuff *before* they start unloading it on everyone else.

Don't be a highly defective boss. Be powerful in a way that's both strong *and* kind.

Don't be a bully boss.

Reflect & Review

The relevant assessment questions for Habit 6 - Bully Bossing - were 16, 17, and 18:

16. My staff knows I care about them as people - not just about their work; sometimes they even open up about their non-work issues.

17. My staff tell me I'm kind and respectful, and they say they enjoy working with me.

18. Even though I'm the boss, people aren't afraid of me; they get stuff done because they understand its importance - not just because I said to do it.

Habit 6 ½
Consistently Inconsistent

Have you ever noticed that many things that make us unhappy actually get less irritating over time? The first scratch of the paint on the new car feels devastating, but we soon learn to live with it, and subsequent dents and dings hardly phase us.

The annoying habits of our partners and kids can also become surprisingly tolerable over time. (When did I become okay with nose-picking?!) You could think of this ability to get used to bad things as our *emotional immune system*. Just like we can fight off diseases, we seem to be able to fight off annoying emotions. Well… sometimes.

There are some things that we never really get used to - stuff that seems to consistently drive us bananas.

Take commuting, for instance. Dan Gilbert, in his excellent book, "Stumbling on Happiness" says commuting is like "a new hell every day." We never really get used to commuting, because it's always something different: Last week someone cut you off; yesterday someone was driving at a snail's pace in the passing lane; today some bone-head was tailgating so closely you actually considered slamming on the breaks and trashing your own car just to teach them a lesson!

Humans have very effective emotional immune systems - we can recover from even the most tragic of life circumstances. But commuting (which on the surface, hardly seems like a tragic life circumstance) consistently makes us unhappy because it changes so fast that we *can't* get used to it.

In other words: We can get used to almost anything, so long as it has some degree of *predictability*.

That brings us to the crux of this (half) habit: consistency. Or rather - the lack thereof.

If things are unpredictable, our emotional immune systems can't help us out. So when a boss is habitually inconsistent, we find ourselves perpetually infuriated.

Habitual Inconsistency?

This final habit of highly defective bosses is distinctly a "half-habit" because it's so irregular. Calling "inconsistency" a *habit* almost seems to be a misnomer.

Semantics of habitual inconsistency aside, we know it's a problem. What does the consistently inconsistent boss look like? As you might imagine, it's hard to predict!

Just when you think you've figured out how to deal with this kind of defective boss, they seem to morph into something else.

Maybe the boss has trouble following through on ideas and seeing efforts through to completion. Maybe they are an emotional cyclone, and you struggle to know whether to joke, get down to business, or brace yourself for an onslaught of criticism. Maybe they flip-flop on what projects seem important or how they want something done.

Perhaps this inconsistent boss has had a change in values. Maybe they were never clear on what was important in the first place.

What does seem clear is that there's often a flurry of confusion and trouble surrounding these inconsistent leaders. As a colleague or as an employee, you may find yourself constantly searching for clarification, bamboozled by what's going on.

The Inconsistent Visionary

If we shift our lens and look at this issue from a boss' perspective, we might be surprised at how they think.

An inconsistent leader may see themselves as a bit of a hero - a fearless visionary, shifting and steering the company to new and exciting places!

Sudden shift in priorities? They'll probably say they were merely responding to forces beyond their control! New management style? They read the latest book! Not sure what to expect? They'll say they like to keep people on their toes.

There is a kernel of truth here. Being flexible, creative, and adaptive are indeed beneficial capacities. In fact, these personalities are highly valued in today's career landscape.

As the pace of change accelerates, we need leaders who can duck, weave, and roll with the punches. We need people who can navigate the stormy seas. We need bosses who are comfortable switching metaphors mid-paragraph!

But this is only one side of the coin.

The other side of the coin is that we also need stability.

If we are seeking the courage to disrupt, *security* is the foundation from which that courage can grow. People are more willing to jump if they have a safety net. The tallest buildings need the strongest foundations. We can better tolerate mixed metaphors if we've started the paragraph with a single-sentence thesis.

The half-habit pattern of consistent inconsistency creates a challenging environment for the staff responsible for bringing ideas to fruition. Visionary leaders who ignore foundations and systems can create a lot of chaos.

In this kind of workplace, employees scramble to accommodate last minute whims and changes and are devastated when they see their nearly-finished projects suddenly get dropped.

Sadly, it's rare for these defective bosses to realize what's going on. It's likely that they are disconnected from the atmosphere they are creating. Many don't see the problem until frustrations reach a boiling point, and even then, they often fail to see themselves as the root cause of the issue.

The Inverted U-Curve of Consistency

Here's another one of my favourite diagrams: The Inverted U-Curve.[126]

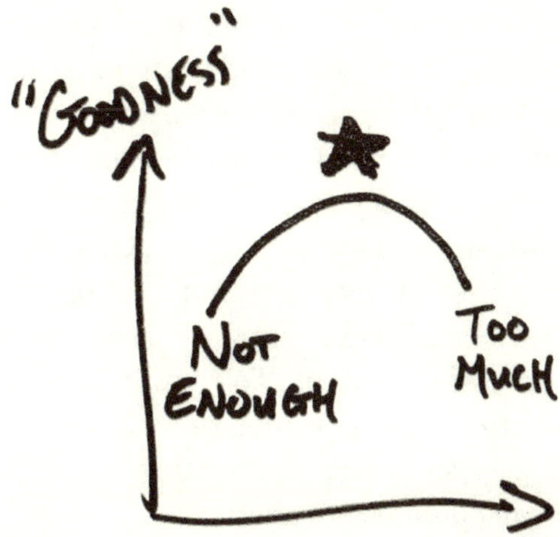

The vertical axis is the "goodness" of the outcome. The horizontal axis represents the *amount* of whatever thing you're thinking about. "Some" of the thing is better than "none" of thing, but "too much" is worse than "some".[127]

So, in our present case, the horizontal axis would represent the degree of *consistency*.

---

[126] These things are so useful. Honestly, I'm a bit shocked we've made it this far *without* one!

[127] I know that sounds a bit vague. It is! That's why it's a diagram! Not *everything* can be represented by inverted U-curves, but a whole lot of stuff can. For instance: "Time spent juggling." Some time is (obviously) better than none, but there is (apparently) such a thing as too much.

We know that *some* consistency is better than none. But *too much* consistency stifles innovation.

The key feature of the inverted U-curve is that there's a hump in the middle! We don't want to be at *either* end of the range.

Higher consistency equates to more stability and predictability. Processes and systems are good!

But, to stay relevant, companies need continual improvement. As technology improves and the world progresses, "doing things the way we've always done them" is a sure-fire recipe for failure. One need only look to the demise of once-dominant companies like Sears, Kodak, or Blockbuster as case-studies in failing to successfully adapt. To remain competitive, there is a constant need to retool, refocus, and rework.

That's why *too much* consistency is problematic - we need *some* openness to change.

On the other hand, the more we push towards innovation, the less predictable things get. The more "new things" we try, the more uncertainty and risk we introduce into our tried and tested methods. We ought not ignore the need for stability. But sadly, defective bosses often *do*.

The message of the inverted U-Curve is simple: When it comes to balancing stability with innovation, the middle ground is the best![128]

---

[128] Or if you want a slightly more playful way to say it, you could try: "The hump is the high point." But I wouldn't recommend using that with your team. On the inverted U-Curve of "using innuendo to make stuff memorable", that phrase probably falls on the "too much" side of the hump.

Development vs Discovery

To find the right *kind* of consistency, effective bosses must strike a balance between the mindset of stability and the mindset of innovation.

One way to think of this is by visualizing a continuum between development and discovery.[129]

The goal of "development", at least in this context, is to improve on things that are already working. Our efforts are often targeted towards making things more efficient and more consistent.[130]

The goal of "discovery" is to find *new* opportunities. Our efforts are targeted at research and exploration.

While our existing products and services pay the bills *today*, we need discovery processes to stay relevant. Perhaps the fruits of our discovery efforts will pay the bills next year, but in the meantime, our

---

129 I've also seen this called The "Exploit-Explore" continuum, but I don't love the "exploit" term.

130 I recognize that "development" is one of those terms that has many definitions, but that's why we're defining it. And it's maybe contextually better than "exploit". And it starts with D, just like discover... so just go with it for now.

development efforts help us build on our current successes right now.

The tension here is that the skills that are needed for good "development" work can be quite different than the skills that make for good "discovery" work.

The path to finding new, innovative ideas requires experimentation. Finding creative solutions requires playing with possibilities and testing things out. Rarely, if ever, can we predict what the best outcome of our efforts will be. Discovery work is *inherently* uncertain and unpredictable.

Venture capitalists (V.C.'s) understand this concept: They invest in a dozen new businesses, expecting half to fail, 5 to do okay, and 1 to hit a home run. To the V.C., each business is like an experiment. If they could predict the home-runs ahead of time, there would be no need to invest in the others. Partial failure was always part of the plan.

Of course, V.C.'s can only do this because they have lots of money. Their financial cushion provides stability.

Let's bring this back to bosses: Managers that are too attached to stability and security will tend to have the habit of Mediocrity Mongering. They'll be extremely consistent, but could benefit from adopting slightly more of the V.C. mindset.

Consistently *inconsistent* bosses are likely thinking *too much* like venture capitalists. Or perhaps they're thinking more like distractable entrepreneurs. Even these folks would do their discovery work better if they were more consistent.

Bottom line: Everyone benefits from finding a balance between consistent systems and flexibility.

Complaints & Confessions

"I worked for a startup, and my boss was constantly late to meetings. He'd brush us off easily, but he seemed to get offended if someone *else* missed a meeting. Maybe he was just high on himself, or maybe he felt like *his* reasons were always valid, but he didn't seem to notice this double standard."

"In my early days of being a manager, I'd read books like crazy - like, a book a week. I was really trying to do a good job and learn as much as I could. And every week I'd be all excited about sharing my new insights with my team. They always listened politely, and nobody ever mentioned it at the time, but 13 years onwards, I now look back at my approach and cringe a bit. It's not that I shouldn't have been reading and learning - that part was helpful, but I probably overwhelmed everyone. They probably didn't say anything because they had tuned out after a few weeks. Why would they pay attention? They knew that next week I'd be onto the next thing anyway."

"I had this one boss who didn't believe in to-do lists. It was so strange. He wanted to be productive, but he said lists felt overwhelming. I mean - I get it. Long lists are overwhelming. But he'd just try to keep everything in his head. And he was bad at it. I think people on the team ended up picking up the slack for him. They'd keep a list of his stuff and constantly check back in with him when he'd forgotten something. I guess we figured it out, but it was annoying. It was like we were playing the role of his parents, and he was a defiant teenager who didn't want to keep track of his own schedule."

"My worst boss was emotionally unhinged. One day she'd be crying about the pressure and tearfully thanking the team for supporting her, and the next day she'd be barking orders at people. Maybe she was just going through a hard time in her life, but she also seemed to have a grudge against some people, so that made everyone feel awkward. I've learned a lot about mental health since then, and I'd bet she had some sort of undiagnosed personality disorder. Or maybe it was diagnosed, but not properly treated? I don't know. I'm not a psychologist. I just know she wasn't well."

Techniques to be Less Terrible

Lighthouse, Not Disco Ball

For teams to function well, they need a clear vision. They need to feel like they're rowing in the same direction.

I heard a nice phrase some years ago: A good leader clarifies what matters most, doesn't say too much, and they repeat themselves a lot.

In other words, it's your job to help everyone cut through the noise and stay focused. Think lighthouse, not disco ball.

A lighthouse is a beacon for guidance. It's a clear, bright, stable marker to help people navigate stormy waters.[131]

Disco balls are different. They scatter a thousand sparkly moving targets across the room. They're pretty, but we certainly don't use them for navigation.

As the boss, do the work to make sure you're crystal clear on what matters most, and make sure everyone can row towards that lighthouse.

80% Development, 20% Discovery

We know we need to balance our time and energy between efficiently managing and growing what we already do (development) and exploring the opportunities that keep us relevant (discovery). But how much effort should we put into each thing?

This will probably depend on your role and the function of your specific team, but let's start with a rough ratio: 80% Development, 20% Discovery. How do we get to this number? We look around and take a guess.

Google was famous for its 20% time, where employees could work one day a week on whatever projects they found interesting. 20% Discovery!

---

[131] Okay… I'm no admiral, but it feels like these days, we are more likely to use radar and GPS and other fancy electronic tools. Yes, the noble lighthouse may be past its prime as a navigational utility, but I'd say it's still in its heyday as a metaphor.

A grad student pal of mine told me his research supervisor had a philosophy: "Always be working on at least two things - one that will definitely work out, and one that probably *won't* work out, but if it did, it would be really amazing. Spend most of your time on the sure bet, but spend a little time nurturing the long shot. Sometimes it'll pay off!"[132]

Do you have to split your time precisely 80-20? Of course not. Adjust the ratio to work for you.[133] And you might not even interpret this tip as a literal splitting of time - perhaps you want to think of it merely as a way to split your *attention*.

Whether it's divided on your calendar or just in your mind, plan to spend about 80% on consistency and refinement and 20% on the higher-risk exploratory ventures.

---

[132] My pal followed this advice in school and in work, but has also followed it in life. He's a super interesting guy. And a bunch of his long-shots have worked out!

[133] Mr. Pareto's 80-20 principle happens to be the same numbers, but just to be clear - it's not quite the same thing. It may well be that 80% of your future success comes from that 20% discovery time you put in, and if it does, *then* we can refer back to Pareto's beans. But it also could turn out that 80% of your success came from one particular part of your "development" work. In that case, the 80-20 rule would still apply, but we'd just be confusing everyone by mixing up the Pareto Principle with the Development-Discovery Ratio. So we'll just put this little confusing tidbit in this footnote and hope nobody mixes it up too badly.

Maximum of Three Priorities

The word "priority" stems from the Latin "prior" which means "first" or "former". Apparently, back in the 14th century when the word entered the English language, it was always used in the singular form. Priority was always the thing that comes first. And you can only have one thing that comes first.

By the 1900's though, the plural "priorities" was showing up more commonly, especially in business. It's like the word has shifted to mean "important stuff". After all, we *do* pursue multiple goals at the same time, and they're all at least somewhat important.

If you ask a highly defective boss to list out their priorities, they're likely to name 7-10 things. If you press them on what matters most, they'll probably tell you that everything needs to be at the top of the list. And as we know, when everything is supposed to be at the top of the list, everything gets done sort of poorly.

It's possible that this lack of *true* prioritization is the reason why that boss is inconsistent and scattered.

If that rings true for you, you might do well to *clarify* your priorities. Here's a simple process:

1. Go ahead and write down the whole list of important stuff.
2. Rank it all out of 10 on the importance scale.
3. Since you probably gave almost everything a 7, 8, or 9, go ahead and put a star beside the three things that actually *truly* matter most.

4. Give yourself permission to make those starred top three things a 10/10, and then make everything else a 6.[134] I know it's hard to demote items, but if you don't do it, you'll probably end up giving everything a 4/10 effort.

Feel too hard to narrow it down to three things? Just remember that a few centuries ago, you would have had to choose just *one* thing.[135] You can do this!

Agendas, Checklists, & Calendars

If you struggle with consistency, you need systems to help you stay focused and stay accountable.

There are all sorts of systems out there, including fancy (and expensive) project management software and CRM programs that are specifically designed to help people manage complex stuff.

If you're dealing with those programs, I tip my hat to you, because you're doing your team a favour. Those systems can be so complex that many people just give up and stop using them altogether.

But if you're a consistently-inconsistent boss, you can be less terrible by starting with the basics.

---

[134] This was a nifty trick a friend told me he read in a book. I didn't invent it, but I decided to try it. Changing the numbers has a profound mental impact!

[135] We might deduce that "renaissance men" were already pushing back on the need to fully commit to a single priority. They clearly *did* have multiple priorities - they just didn't have a word for it.

Here are three basic systems that you probably need in some form or another.

1. **Agendas.** I'm not only talking about meeting agendas, though those are one form. An agenda is essentially a running project list. You may want to have an agenda with each of your direct reports, or you may want to consolidate it somehow. But it's helpful to have a place to put the ideas you know you need to discuss. Don't rely on your brain.
2. **Checklists.** Need to *remember* something? Consider a checklist. Have a set of things that you do *routinely*? Consider a checklist. Putting stuff on a list is not a sign of weakness; it's a sign of wisdom and experience. Professionals use these things all the time. Pilots use checklists before *every* flight to make sure all the systems are working before they get in the air.[136] Surgeons literally have checklists of the items they use in surgery, right down to the number of sponges they use.[137] Your brain is good at lots of things, but consistently remembering long lists of stuff is not one of them.

---

[136] "Wait... weren't *you* in charge of refuelling?..."

[137] Apparently surgeons do the checklist twice - at the beginning and again at the end. Why? Because before they did that, sponges would occasionally get left inside a person. Those were probably bad days for everyone involved.

3. **Calendars.** Believe it or not, I've met professionals who do not keep any sort of calendar - they try to keep it all in their head. This is a bad idea, and doubly so if you're a boss. You're coordinating schedules, arranging meetings, and you'll also need to block time for *your* important stuff. Whether you're digital or analog (paper-based), give your brain some relief and use a calendar to track meetings and organize your time.

Here's the theme: Systems are very important. The best systems are the ones that *work* that you actually *use.*[138]

Make It Visual

When people feel scattered, they need clarity. They need to know where to focus. They need to see the bigger picture.

Notice that all of those phrases reference vision: Clarity. Focus. Seeing. Making things visual is one of my favourite approaches to help unify the team and provide the needed clarity and focus. In our world of information overload, an aspiring less-terrible boss can look for ways to simplify ideas for those in their orbit. Here are a few visual ideas:

- **Online Whiteboards.** These are great collaborative tools. Everyone can contribute

[138] I'll spare you the Venn diagram...

at the same time. Many have pre-set templates to help guide your thinking.[139]

- **Infographics.** There's a reason that infographics became popular: They make it easier for people to understand stuff. A well-designed infographic communicates just what people need to know, and it does it in a way that relieves some of the mental load.
- **Back-of-the-napkin Sketches.** These things are famous because they work. If you can say it so simply it fits on a napkin, you're on the right track. Venn diagrams, inverted U-Curves, a 2x2 Matrix... it's the type of stuff that gets me excited![140]
- **Your Personal Dashboard.** A car's "dashboard" is designed to give you all the info you need to drive the car safely - but not so much info that it's overwhelming or confusing. We can steal this concept and create our own *personal* dashboard. I use a whiteboard in my office, but you could use electronic ones also. I include my big areas

---

[139] Our team likes Canva whiteboards, but there are a bunch of online platforms. Try them out and see what works and what people like using.

[140] The key with back-of-the-napkin sketches is that they need to be both simple *and* compelling. It's a 2x2 matrix. Simple & not-compelling at least gets you a clear "no". Complex & compelling is not bad, but your lunch mate doesn't want an essay on a napkin. If your back-of-napkin sketch is complex and *also* not-compelling, you might need to start from scratch... and also you might need to start looking for a new lunch mate.

of responsibility, including my home and family life. Design it however you like, but the key is to make it visual. At a glance, we want to be able to ensure we're not neglecting important stuff.

You know the old saying: A picture is worth a thousand words.[141] So make your stuff visual. Visual tools help you *and* your team. You'll become a better communicator, and it'll help you stay clear and consistent.

Final Words on Habit 6 ½

Some bosses, especially entrepreneurs, tend to feel comfortable in the realm of high uncertainty.

Highly defective inconsistent bosses are impossible to predict. They cause chaos as they ping-pong from one idea to the next, leaving the team left behind to pick up the broken pieces and half-done projects. They may be emotionally unstable. They are often scatterbrained rebels. They may resist structure in the name of creative freedom.

The aspiring less-terrible boss knows that organizations need to find the right *balance* of structure and freedom to thrive. *Some* consistency is good, but too much will kill innovation.

They give the team a strong, clear vision. They are like a lighthouse - a beacon toward which staff can

---

[141] Isn't it ironic that there's no picture to go along with this phrase?

direct their efforts. They communicate a small number of clear priorities, but they carve out space for exploratory ideas and experimental projects.

Most importantly, they model the balance between predictability and openness; the less-terrible boss will use enough systems to keep themselves organized, but they also give themselves enough freedom to imagine new possibilities.

Don't be a highly defective boss. Provide enough stability to support your team's lofty aspirations.

Don't be consistently inconsistent.

Reflect & Review

The relevant assessment questions for Habit 6 ½ - Consistently Inconsistent - were 19, 20, and 21:

19. My staff would say I'm highly reliable because I actually follow through on what I say I will do. (And if I don't, I apologize.)

20. I know that innovation is important but it can be messy, so I make lots of effort to create stability for our team.

21. Even when I have great new ideas, I try to avoid sudden changes to important projects; pivoting too fast or too often can create chaos.

Bonus Round: At Least We're Not *That* Terrible

In all my conversations about bad bosses, there were a few stories that stood out. They may technically fit as examples of one habit or another, but they seemed so striking that they needed a category of their own.

Perhaps you'll enjoy reading them. Maybe they'll make you cringe.

But hopefully you can take solace in the fact that while these stories are *true*, they are also *rare*.

So… you know… at least we're not *that* terrible.

Mafia Boss

"When I was in my 30's - more than 50 years ago now - I was running a small non-profit, and I had a deal with a company to do some accounting work for them in exchange for the use of some office space.

"Turns out the company owner - my boss - was in the mafia. One day I actually overheard him talking about 'concrete shoes' with someone on the phone… as in: '*Maybe they'll find you at the bottom of the lake in your fancy new concrete shoes.*'

"He was sitting in a high-back chair looking out the window, and I think he had forgotten I was in the room working at my desk. I tiptoed out of there, grabbed the secretary and whispered: 'We need to go for coffee... Right. Now.'

"I got three blocks away, found a payphone, and called the police.

"They put protections in place for the guy who he'd threatened, so that was a relief.

"And then I started planning how to get myself out of that job without tipping anyone off about what I knew. I never talked about that much, for obvious reasons.

"Anyway, I'd say that that guy qualified as a fairly bad boss."

A Short Story that Says Enough

"Bad boss? Yep - I had one.

"He slapped my rear end."

Temper Tantrum

"I worked at a camp, and this one boss had a terrible temper. Physically, he was enormous. He'd once fought in the Yugoslavian war as a solider, and he was a martial arts expert, though apparently he missed the anger-management part.

"He once (mistakenly) thought I had overturned a decision he made. A co-worker warned me he was mad, and looking for me.

"I suddenly remembered two awkward interactions I'd had with the guy. Once, he interrupted my staff training to share a story of how he had beaten up one of his employees - badly enough to put him in the hospital. Another day, the wacko had waved a combat knife around, saying, 'This is how we solve problems in the real world.'

"Sure enough, he showed up with his fists clenched and shoulders all puffed out like he was going to beat me up. He came after me - getting closer and closer.

"I just kept moving away from him and repeating 'I didn't do it - I don't have the authority to make that choice.' It was like a game of cat and mouse. My coworker stayed around, which was good, because if I had been killed, at least there'd have been a witness.

"He kept on shouting obscenities, trying to get in my face, fists ready at his belt-line. I just kept retreating.

"Eventually - thankfully - he stormed away.

"Traumatizing. He never apologized... never even talked about it, though he did offer me some time off. Maybe he realized he crossed a line?

"I took a leave of absence as soon as I could get a ride out of there. And I didn't go back.

Onwards: The Less-Terrible Boss

When I interviewed for my first jobs, way back in my final year of university, I distinctly remember feeling a sense of awe - or maybe it was admiration - for the bosses sitting on the other side of the table.

They were older than me. They already *had* jobs. They probably had houses and cars and money in their bank accounts. They were powerful enough that they were hiring people!

I don't think I *consciously* thought about any of that stuff, but it was all there under the surface, in a tangled web of assumptions. Whatever I *was* thinking about (probably it involved how to impress them while showing off my engineering skills in a polished but not-too-desperate sort of way), there was one thing that I was definitely *not* thinking: "This boss-person across from me is a *regular person.*"

It never dawned on me, for instance, that this guy had possibly been on my side of the table just 18 months earlier.

It didn't occur to me that the woman across the table was perhaps also a mom, and that she had very likely spent her morning wrestling kids into snowsuits, unsuccessfully coaxing them to finish their half-eaten bananas, and narrowly averting a fist fight in the back seat, all before dropping them off at school, late again.

I certainly never wondered whether this fellow wearing a suit ever argued with his spouse or visited his hospitalized dad or spent stressful hours reviewing his family finances to make sure the February mortgage payment didn't bounce.

Never thought once about any of it! I was fully focused on my *own* life transition: growing from a student into a "working adult". I was still several years away from the realization that working adults - regular people - sometimes become bosses.

Would My Boss Have Changed Things?

Even when I became an employee in my first "real job" after graduating, I felt like I was sort of playing pretend.

My boss wasn't terrible. At least, I don't *think* he was. He was fine. I didn't get much of a welcome... a quick orientation, I guess. That didn't offend me, because he was *always* busy. I didn't want to be a burden for him.

There was a lot to learn, and I got a few scattered training sessions from him and a few other supervisors, but I remember struggling to stay awake. Even after a few weeks, I didn't really feel like I had a sense of what I was building towards. And I didn't feel like I could contribute anything yet. I sort of felt like I was muddling my way along - putting in my hours.

I didn't last long in the corporate world as an employee - just four weeks. Which isn't even really true… because I was on vacation for one of the weeks.

Was it my *boss'* fault? Honestly, I didn't think of it that way at the time. He was probably doing his best. He was a good guy.

It was certainly at least partially *my* fault. I definitely didn't know what I was doing. I knew I had skills, but I didn't know what questions to ask. Most importantly, I didn't tell people I was seriously considering leaving. I kept it all inside.

Could my boss have coaxed any of this out of me? Maybe.

I felt like the world of work - or at least the job I had landed - wasn't a good fit for me and my skillset. Databases, I guess, weren't my thing. I liked teaching. I liked working with people. I made up my mind that I wanted to go back to grad school. I thought I could stick it out at work for six or nine months, but I figured (or hoped?) that by then I'd be useful. Leaving at *that* point would have more of an impact. So, I reasoned that it would be "kinder" for me to just quit immediately and let them find an employee that actually fit.

But I admit I'd hardly started… Would I have felt differently if my onboarding had been stronger? Maybe.

When I resigned, my boss and his colleagues were genuinely surprised. They asked if I would reconsider. They asked if I'd be more interested in another department of the company. I didn't actually *know* if I'd like something different, because it was all new to me anyway. Dealing with stock markets would have been a lot different than dealing with databases where I started. But I'd already made up my mind. I was leaving.

But would I have given it more consideration if my interests had been brought up proactively? Or my learning goals? Or my career development plans? Definitely.

Bosses Are People Too

In my work with management teams across the continent, I am constantly witness to a simple truth: We're all humans.

Bosses really *are*, at least usually, regular people: They have lives outside of work and hobbies that have fallen by the wayside. They have friends and families, and they've experienced the joys of love and the grief of loss. They have health challenges of their own. They have career aspirations of their own. They have *bosses* of their own.

Maybe some of those bosses, like me, sort of stumbled into being a boss. Maybe, like me, they hadn't thought that much about how to do it. Maybe, like me, some of them didn't even *realize* they'd become a boss.

I'm not sure when this all started to click for me, but things look different now than they did at age 23. And I'm 100% certain that the next few decades will bring still more perspective.

I've met some multi-millionaire high-status bosses in person. They're so normal-seeming that I've often only found out after-the-fact. Even so, I still catch myself making assumptions about other people in high-status positions. I sometimes wonder what it'd be like to be a gazillionaire tech CEO or a famous celebrity. No doubt "those people" face a variety of unique problems, but my wise-self knows there's a good chance that we share much more in common than my daydreaming would suggest.

In other words, I feel like my present-day self sees a lot more common humanity in other people than I used to. Even successful bosses are people too.

Kind, Fun, & Generous

Here's a question for you: How do *you* want to be remembered as a boss?

Years ago, during one of my New Year's Day goal-setting reflection activities, I was thinking about our small company, and a phrase came to mind:

"Happy, proud, grateful team."

That described how I wanted others to feel, which was a good start. It got me thinking about what *I* needed to do - who I needed to *be* - to create that. I wrote down another phrase:

"Kind, fun, & generous CEO."

Embarrassingly, it wasn't *that* many years ago... I probably should have thought about it sooner, because these few simple words have proven to be super-helpful. I jotted both phrases on my whiteboard as a reminder.

When I'm in a bind, I sometimes glance over and see if my phrases offer me any clarity. They often do.

Am I *always* kind, fun, and generous? Nope.

Frankly, sometimes I'm annoying, grouchy, and fretting about our finances. On those days, I'm probably a terrible boss. Some days my family needs me so urgently that I have to cancel everything and throw wrenches into my team's plans. Those days can feel pretty terrible too.

But, hey - it's all empathy-building. Life can be tough. My staff probably have some terrible days too. We all do!

And let's face it: As important as work is, and as important as bosses are, our work-selves are just one *part* of our human lives. I just hope my kind, fun, generous side - the version of me that's *learning* how to be better - the *less*-terrible one - can show up when it counts. I'm the boss, after all... maybe I can make things a bit easier for the people around me.

Aspiring for Greatness

Bosses matter. They make companies better. They make people's *lives* better.

Being a boss - and thinking about how to be better at it - has made *my* life better. Leading a team has been one of the most rewarding aspects of my career.

Truthfully, I started this book because I knew it would make *me* better. But actually writing it has convinced me that better bosses can make the *whole world* better.

I get it. We all have *limited* time, and it's impossible to be great at *everything*. But I think this better-boss thing is a worthy pursuit.

Let's aspire for boss-level greatness, even if it sometimes feels like "less-terrible" is the best we can be.

Appendix: A Week in the Life

Let's try putting this all together. Suppose you lead a team of seven people. They're good folks. You were shoulder-tapped to manage the team after your boss moved on two years ago. What might a week look like?

Sunday

Fresh off reading a book about being a better boss,[142] you decide to take an hour or so after the kids are in bed to look ahead to the upcoming week.

You grab a blank piece of paper and draw out the 2x2 matrix of boss functions from Habit 1.

Team Dynamics... Things are pretty good. No action needed here.

Career Development... *Are people fulfilled?* This seems more awkward to assess. You realize you don't actually know. You've never asked. Maybe that's step one. You decide to try a casual approach - you'll make a point of having conversations with each teammate over a coffee sometime in the next month.

Vision & Strategy... You feel moderately confident that you're prioritizing well, but you don't know if your *whole team* would be able to clearly state

---

[142] I heard it was a *really* good book.

the three big picture projects and how they relate to the company's overall strategy. Even though you want to minimize meetings, you decide to *add* another 30-minute "Strategy Check-in" meeting for Wednesday.

Project Implementation... Things are good, but your weekly meetings feel sort of unfocused. Are they strategy meetings or project meetings? Oh... they mix both. That's the problem. You make up a quick agenda, making sure you're sticking to questions that focus on the short term, project-based work:

1. What did you work on last week?
2. What do you want the team to know?
3. What's your top priority for this week, and do you foresee any roadblocks?

Monday

You start your day with some productive work time - two hours on your most important project.

Your weekly check-in meeting comes next.

"Hey - I'd love to try a new agenda for our check-in meetings. I've had the sense that these meetings are taking longer than they need to..." You realize it *could* sound like you're blaming everyone else, and you don't want to be a *finger pointer*, so you clarify. "If the meetings run long, that's *my* fault, since I'm the one facilitating. I know we have lots to talk about, but to help us stay focused, I've added a separate meeting for Wednesday to talk about the bigger picture quarterly plans."

You start in on your agenda, and as people share what they worked on, you remember the importance of recognition. You don't feel like you were ever a *credit stealer*, but you make an extra effort to say a genuine "thank you" after each person shares their week's accomplishments.

In the conversation about people's roadblocks, only one person brings up a problem. "I've found an app that would handle the issue, but it costs $12," they explain.

You seize the opportunity to talk about *de-hassling* and the *$50 Magic Pill*: "You know what? You're all smart people - and your time is valuable. If you can save yourself a big nuisance and a couple hours by spending twelve bucks, that feels like a no-brainer to me - do it! In fact, let's make it an informal rule on our team: If you can save yourself a hassle by spending some money - let's set the limit at 50 bucks for now - then you've got my permission to do it. No need to get advanced clearance, but let's say you need to let the team know at the next meeting. That'll help me keep a handle on what sort of problems people are facing."

Your team likes the idea.

Before the meeting ends, you remember the *Next Action Go-Round* and decide to give it a try. Sure enough, two questions emerge about target deadlines and which part of the project is more urgent. You realize it was a case of *fuzzy expectations*. You feel a bit frustrated, and your *instinct* is to ask why this didn't this come up before now. But you resist the urge to "point the finger" and instead say, "Great questions! And that's my fault for not helping us get more clarity sooner."

The problems get sorted, and you end the meeting seven minutes early.

Tuesday

After yesterday's meeting, you were reflecting on your teammate - the one who found the $12 app to solve her problem. Not only does she regularly identify roadblocks, but she *also* seems to proactively find solutions. You don't want to "rank" your team members - everyone has some great skills - but you have to admit that she's your go-to person for important clients. Plus, she's a real joy to work with. You realize that she is one of your *star performers*.

Just as importantly, you realize that it's been over nine months since you had a 1-on-1 conversation with her, and you have no idea what her career goals are or if she's happy with her role.

You decide to make a quick phone call to her. "Hi! I know I'm calling out of the blue - but I had two things for you: Firstly, I just wanted to tell you how appreciative I am of the work you're doing. I was thinking about it yesterday and I realized I don't say it enough. Thank you! You're really adding a ton of value to the team."

She seems a bit surprised. "Oh?! Umm.. thanks! Are you going to start the next sentence with, 'But...'? Am I about to get fired?"

"No, no!" You reassure her. "The second thing was that I realized that I haven't actually *asked* about your career goals in a long time. I don't want to lose you from our team, of course, but a superstar like you is going to have ambitions. I know I haven't always been the best boss, but I'd love to be part of your plan rather than being oblivious to it. Anyway - maybe we could set up a lunch meeting next week?"

She seems thrilled - and also re-assured. "I'd love to. And thanks for those kind words. It means a lot. I mean, I always try to do good work, but sometimes I get a bit insecure about whether I'm doing as well as I should."

You get the lunch date set and feel good about the conversation. You remind yourself: *Water the tall poppies.*

Wednesday

Today's the day for that new strategy meeting. Since you know it's a new thing for everyone, you start by giving people some context: "I don't want to add more meetings if they're not necessary, but I was thinking about whether I'd done a good enough job at clarifying our department's strategy."

You realize this is actually a chance to *ask for collaborative input and feedback.*

"Here's the first question I have for all of you: When it comes to our team's big projects, what information am I sharing well, and what information do you wish I was sharing better?"

You make a point of giving an example to help reinforce that you're open to talking about your shortcomings. "For instance, I don't think I've communicated about why some projects get so much more funding than others."

You know that giving people time to think is helpful, and you don't want the loudest teammate to take up all the airtime, so you structure the discussion: "Take a moment to jot down a few ideas, and then we'll go around the circle!"

To your delight, people *do* share their honest thoughts. Most comments are positive, with a few questions and a few tips for improving.

But then one person candidly shares some feedback that does *not* feel good: "Honestly, I think you're a bit scattered. I don't know *which* projects matter most - let alone our strategy... We're doing *a lot*, and it seems like *you* keep changing your mind."

You feel a pang of embarrassment and shame. You *do* feel like you're scattered sometimes. You make a note to discuss with your therapist. You *want* to snip back at the guy, and you wish *he'd* read the part of the bosses book about strong and kind. But, you realize that this is a critical moment of truth: The team is offering their genuine feedback, and they'll be watching closely to see how you respond to it. You take a breath and decide that the best strong and kind thing *you* can do in the moment is to validate how he's feeling.

"You know, I can see that for sure. Thanks for being so honest." You remember that *reality testing* is a good way to test your assumptions. Maybe *everyone* thinks you're scattered, but maybe it's *just that one guy*? You ask the team! "Are others feeling like I change my mind too often?"

There's a good discussion. A few people actually come to your defense - empathizing and saying that they think you're doing your best to manage a lot of projects, but they sort of agree that they don't really see how to think about everything all at once. Even the original attacker softens and says that this meeting *has* been helpful in clearing things up. Still, your "Team Dynamics" radar senses there might be something brewing here. You make a note to follow-up 1-on-1 to make sure he feels like he was heard and ask if anything is lingering.

You end by reinforcing everyone's contributions and taking responsibility! "Honestly, thank you for all this - it was an awesome start to the discussion, and my takeaway is that I *do* need to be more transparent about sharing our big picture priorities. I've written down your other comments and questions, but instead of discussing them now, which would put us overtime, I'll put another meeting on the schedule for next week."

Thursday

You spend the morning working on a draft of a digital whiteboard to represent the different projects the team is working on. So far, the team has been using spreadsheets to manage and list the various projects, but yesterday's meeting helped you see that a *visual* representation might be better.

In drafting the whiteboard, you start to see a challenge. There are way too many projects. That's probably why the spreadsheets are messy. *Lighthouse, not disco-ball* - you remind yourself.

You figure this would be a perfect chance to check in with the teammate who said you were scattered. You don't want to delay talking about potential team dynamics issues, and you also want to show him you were serious about working on the problem! You jump on a video call.

"Hey! I wanted to follow up about yesterday. I think your comments about having too many projects were spot on."

He seems surprised by this. "Oh? Really?"

"Yeah. I'm working on a visual that I think could help, and I wanted to get your opinion on it." You also need to be strong and kind, so you had rehearsed how to say this next bit a few times. "But I also wanted to check in - you seemed a bit frustrated in the meeting yesterday, and I wanted to ask if you had more to share. Are you upset with me? Or someone else on the team? You do good work, so it's important to me to hear your concerns."

He smiles and chuckles. "No, but thanks for asking. I think I was too harsh on you yesterday - sorry about that. I was frustrated with some stuff going on at home."

"Ahh... I'm sorry to hear it, and thanks for the apology. Is there anything I can do?"

"No, no. Our car was in the shop - big repair bill. That, and I had to renew my driver's license the day before... it was a total hassle. It's all fine - I was just annoyed."

Don't neglect the people-part of the job - prioritize relationships - you mentally remind yourself. You spend a few moments commiserating, and he seems genuinely okay. You get back to task-based thinking. "I still need your help. Here's my issue: We're working on *nine* projects. But that feels like way too many for people to get their heads around. We're supposed to have *three priorities maximum*."

"So you're looking for a way to cut six projects?"

"No... it's not that simple. I need a way to help people understand how these nine projects fit together and get prioritized."

You chat a bit more, sharing ideas, and at one point, he asks a question about how things are budgeted. You realize that your budgeting aligns with the typical balance between *development and discovery*!

"You know, 80% of our budget goes to our two current best-seller products. Come to think of it, those really are priorities 1 and 2."

He asks a simple question: "So what about our other 7 projects?"

You get to explain some of the context: "Well, our team is also involved with *new* product experimentation - that's the other 20% of our budget. And that 20% is spread over 6 or 7 small projects at a time."

He chimes in again: "Ah - so that's why they seem so random."

"Yeah, but our job is to figure out *which* random small project we think can become a real winner. Actually, now that I think of it this way, *that* seems like priority number 3!"

You quickly re-arrange the whiteboard to show the three priorities. Priority 1 - Best-seller 1. Priority

2 - Best-seller 2. Priority 3 - "Find the best prospect". You group the list of 7 "discovery" projects under Priority 3.

"Obviously this is an *SFD - a Crappy First Draft.* We've got lots of sub-projects we could fill in under Priorities 1 and 2 also, but maybe we'll get more buy-in on this tool by letting everyone fill things in and suggest their tweaks? In the meantime - thanks for the input! What do *you* think of this visual? Does seeing things grouped this way help you see why some of our small projects always get less funding? And why they end up taking a back seat to the bigger projects if there are urgent deadlines?"

Your colleague does the eyebrows-up and gentle nodding thing that suggests he might be having an ah-ha moment.

Friday

Friday starts off with you making some plans to give compliments to your team more regularly - *systematizing the recognition.* Next month is the annual company picnic, and you decide that'd be a good occasion to give everyone a short handwritten note.

You also want to do something publicly, and there's a project debrief meeting coming up next week, so you plan to start that one with a few words about each person's unique contributions.

You get a phone call from one of your newer teammates. She seems flustered and shares some bad news - an important client gave them some less-than-satisfied feedback.

"Gosh - that's tricky." You remember *not* to jump in and make suggestions too fast. "*How can I help?* Do you want me to make a decision here? Or we could work through it together? Or did you already have a plan and you just wanted to let me know?"

She thinks for a moment. "Well, I guess I could make the decision, but I'm not sure I have the authority. I know you talked about spending up to 50 bucks to solve a problem, but this would be more like five *hundred* - every *year*! The issue is our software. I think we've outgrown it. I mean, it's manageable, but we've sort of jerry-rigged it to do what we need. Honestly, I'm surprised this issue hasn't shown up with *more* clients."

You realize she's telling you about the hassle of working with *shoddy tools*. "Okay - I didn't realize it was causing so many issues! That software package is something we use every day, and if it's giving us issues, we need a tool that works! I'll talk to my boss."

She seems a bit relieved, but then unloads a bit more. "I'm really sorry! I should have caught the problem before... I know the client is a big one. I feel really badly."

You know this is another moment of truth. "Don't worry about it. You've only been with us six months - you're doing your best!" You remember to *start by taking responsibility*. "I didn't catch it either, and I've been overseeing the project for way longer, so don't be too hard on yourself. I think I can do better at asking questions to help people proactively spot these types of problems. But either way, what matters right now is what we should *do* now."

She seems relieved, and she suggests a plan that sounds reasonable to you.

You remember the *"Enthusiastically Re-hire Test"*. You'd *definitely* re-hire her. Yes, she slipped up, but she took responsibility and identified a deeper issue - it wasn't really *her* fault. She's been fantastic. You make a mental note to check back with her next week to make sure she knows how much you appreciate her.

Later that afternoon, she sends you a text message: "I talked with the client - we've sorted it out. Thanks for being so understanding earlier today. My boss at my last job would have yelled at me and thrown a big fit."

Saturday

As you walk the grocery store aisles, you find yourself thinking about that nice text message.

Okay, being compared to her former fit-throwing *bully boss* seems like a low bar, but then again, she didn't have to say *anything*.

You realize that you don't get *tons* of praise from your team, but you *do* get occasional texts and thank you's like that one. And, hey! The only *critical* comment of the week came with a next-day apology!

You know you shouldn't pin your professional success to the number of grateful text messages you get, but those moments of appreciation *do* feel good.

You think back to when you started on the team - two years before you got shoulder-tapped to be the manager. Your boss was good! Did you *ever* say thanks to her? You can't remember doing it even once. It never occurred to you that bosses might benefit from a bit of positive reinforcement.

Somewhere between the soup aisle and the dairy section, you pull your shopping cart next to a freezer and decide to send that old boss a text message of your own:

"Hey! Long time... almost 2 years actually! I'm still in the manager role you got me into... this boss stuff is really tricky! I read this book about bad bosses last week, and it helped me see that you were a really GREAT boss to work for! Thanks for caring about us as people - not just as workers. You managed to encourage high-standards, help remove obstacles to get us there, and when we did, you always shared the credit! Even when I messed up, I never felt scared to bring things up, and our career conversations really helped me understand myself better and clarify my goals! Anyway... I don't think I ever really said thanks, so... thanks for being a great role model!"

Acknowledgements

In 2019, I wrote an article series about bad bosses. The feedback was incredibly encouraging; folks told me they liked the ideas, and they said they wanted more. I decided it should be a book, and here it is. But it didn't happen without help.

Katharine Snider-McNair, my original article editor, was instrumental in forming these ideas.

Calder Hutchinson and Brandon Love were my primary editors. If you liked the jokes, thank them. If you didn't, you can blame me. Either way, the ideas I tried to convey in these pages are clearer and more powerful because of those two friends.

Countless people shared their stories and (often-sordid) experiences. They brought the book to life.

My team at Beanstalk Creative deserve a big trophy for managing the day-to-day of our training company while I tuned out the world to write, sometimes for days at a time.

Sebastian Jaster is my go-to illustrator and cover designer, and his brilliance once again shines through. David Moses did the audiobook production, and he made me sound better than I do in real life.

My amazing wife Kathleen was exceptionally gracious with affording me the writing time.

Our three amazing kids were less-gracious, but they did their best.

Mostly, thanks to *you* for caring enough to read it. The world needs good ~~bosses~~ people. Let's go do it!

Recommended Resources

American Psychological Association. (2023). *Work in America: Workplace health and well-being*. Retrieved from https://www.apa.org/pubs/reports/work-in-america/2023-workplace-health-well-being

American Psychological Association. (n.d.). *Multitasking*. Retrieved from https://www.apa.org/topics/research/multitasking

Bellet, C., De Neve, J.-E., & Ward, G. (2019). Does employee happiness have an impact on productivity? *Saïd Business School Working Paper 2019-13*. Retrieved from SSRN: https://ssrn.com/abstract=3470734

Bryson, A., & MacKerron, G. (2017). Are you happy while you work? *The Economic Journal, 127*(599), 106-125. https://doi.org/10.1111/ecoj.12269

Chartered Management Institute. (2023). *Taking responsibility: Why UK PLC needs better managers.*

Easton, G. S., & Jarrell, S. L. (1998). The effects of total quality management on corporate performance: An empirical investigation. *The Journal of Business, 71*(2), 253-307. https://doi.org/10.1086/209744

Gallup & Workhuman. (2023). *The human-centered workplace: Building organization cultures that thrive.*

Harter, J. K., Hayes, T. L., & Schmidt, F. L. (2002). Business-unit-level relationship between employee satisfaction, employee engagement, and business outcomes: A meta-analysis. *Journal of Applied Psychology, 87*(2), 268-279. https://doi.org/10.1037/0021-9010.87.2.268

Punishment doesn't work. (2014, January 3). *Psychology Today*. Retrieved from https://www.psychologytoday.com/ca/blog/feeling-our-way/201401/punishment-doesnt-work

Wickman, G. (2007). *Traction: Get a grip on your business*. BenBella Books.

Yule, S., Yule, J., & Arthur, C. (2025). Turning stress into success—Surgery as professional sport. *JAMA Surgery*. Advance online publication. https://doi.org/10.1001/jamasurg.2024.60

www.ingramcontent.com/pod-product-compliance
Lightning Source LLC
LaVergne TN
LVHW100312210926
848480LV00003B/1104

* 9 7 8 1 0 6 9 6 3 9 5 0 9 *